07

A Secret History of the Bangkok Hilton

OTHER BOOKS BY THE SAME AUTHORS

BY CHAVORET JARUBOON

The Last Executioner (2006)

BY PORNCHAI SEREEMONGKONPOL

Ladyboys (2008)

A SECRET HISTORY OF THE BANGKOK HILTON

by **Chavoret Jaruboon**
and **Pornchai Sereemongkonpol**

MAVERICK HOUSE PUBLISHERS.

Published by Maverick House, Unit 19 Dunboyne Business Park,
Dunboyne, Co. Meath, Ireland.

www.maverickhouse.com
email: info@maverickhouse.com

ISBN: 978-1-905379-71-2

5 4 3 2 1

The paper used in this book comes from wood pulp of managed forests.
For every tree felled at least one tree is planted, thereby renewing natural
resources.

Acknowledgements ❧

First and foremost, I would like to say *kob khun* to all at Maverick House Publishers, and Khun Pornchai in particular, for helping me prepare my second English book.

I also owe a debt of gratitude to people Pornchai and I interviewed for this book. Your insights are very valuable in showing different aspects of Thai penology and Bang Kwang.

Last, but not least, my wife Tew for sticking with me in sickness and in health.

Dedication ❧

If any good comes from this book, I would like it to be for those who have shared their stories, and those whose lives I mention in this book.

INTRODUCTION

When I was a boy, my father made it our custom to leave our home in Bangkok every weekend to visit our relatives in Nonthaburi province. The province adjoins Bangkok, the capital of Thailand, and in those days, the best way to travel there was by water.

As we floated down the Chao Phraya River, I was mesmerised by the liveliness that surrounded me: Buddhists released turtles and fish into the river to 'make merit' or improve their karma; boys with mischievous smiles jumped off the banks; rafts of water hyacinth formed little green islands here and there; fish surfaced looking for the treats people threw them, causing countless ripples to glisten playfully in the sunlight. All that went on was captivating to me. Seen through my young and naive eyes, the world was full of joy and wonder then. Little did I know what an illusion that would turn out to be.

Por (father) and I usually arrived at Nonthaburi pier on Sunday mornings. From there we continued on foot to my uncle's house, which happened to be next door to the notorious Bang Kwang Central Prison, also known as the Bangkok Hilton or Big Tiger.

The Bangkok Hilton is a maximum-security prison for inmates who have been sentenced to more than 30 years in jail or have received the death penalty. It is the tiger that either devours you entirely or spits out what is left after it has feasted on you in captivity. It is the most feared prison in Thailand.

As we walked past, I would stare from a distance at the electrified barbed wire fencing topping the prison wall. Guards with machine guns stood inside the towers that formed part of the wall. I wondered what was going on in there and whether the people would be able ever to get out. I never imagined I would have those questions answered—and much more besides.

To Thai minds, the Bangkok Hilton is a place of gloom and danger. Years later, I found out that working there was a risky business for those who lacked moral courage as there were plenty of opportunities to be corrupt.

Life gradually introduced me to good and evil until I realised how grey the world actually is and always will be. This is especially true in Thailand, where many things are 'flexible' or 'compromised' and a blind eye can be turned when money is paid or power is exercised. A lot of things in Thailand don't always work the way they should.

Once as my father and I were on our way to visit my uncle, we came across a team of barefoot prisoners in their tattered brown uniforms cleaning the sun-parched road. I couldn't imagine how thick their soles must be to endure the heat of the ground. They had been brought out of the prison for a few hours to labour under the glaring midday blaze.

The practice of prisoners performing public service can be traced back hundreds of years and continues to this day. During the early days of Rattanakosin, Thailand's current era, they contributed to the kingdom by building canals, roads and railroads among other public structures. In fact, the Bangkok Hilton was built in part with prison labour.

During World War I, the Corrections Department transferred 200 prisoners from Bang Kwang Prison to a temporary camp in the Bang Khen area and ordered them to grow rice and raise livestock to be sold cheaply to law-abiding citizens. At that time, Thailand was suffering economically and such commodities were scarce.

The practice was revised in 1980 and a set of rules was introduced. Convicts are entitled to reductions in their sentences equal to the number of days they have performed public service and, on some occasions, a small wage.

The intention is to remind people that prisoners are not outcasts but are still part of society and that they can contribute towards the common good. Personally I don't think it really influences Thai attitudes towards inmates.

In fact, this arrangement has backfired a few times as prisoners have attempted to escape.

As a boy, I saw the convicts as bogeymen rather than outcasts. At that first close encounter, they were figures to be feared. Yet I could hardly take my eyes off them. This left a lasting impression on me. The difference between then and now is that I've adopted a more realistic attitude.

The scraping sounds the ankle shackles made as they struggled to walk and work further drew my attention to them. One inmate had covered his swarthy body with tattoos of tigers, Hanuman, the Hindu monkey god, and occult writing. The prisoners derived great feelings of support and protection from these. They did so, perhaps, because there wasn't much else for them to hold on to. One could easily wonder why, if the inked symbols possessed any power, those men had ended up in jail.

Today's prisons offer the inmates much more than hard labour. There are opportunities to take part in productive activities such as playing music, joining in with religious groups, undertaking vocational training and education. Even so, some choose to busy themselves with narcotics, money-making schemes, gambling and killing for cash in order to make the long days spent in captivity and the harsh living conditions bearable. Some have to deal with the additional anxiety of being on death row or the prospect of spending the rest of their lives rotting in prison.

Of course, the inmates could not undertake such activities if the guards didn't let them. Putting a stop to such things, however, would mean losing the monthly kickbacks the inmates in charge dutifully pass on to guards.

I suppose any child would have experienced the mixed feelings of fear and curiosity I did on first encountering those strange, ragged fellows whom the adults used to frighten us. There were also prison guards standing sternly nearby. One of them caught me staring at him and I quickly turned my gaze away. I grabbed onto my father's shirt tightly as we sped up.

On the way home, my father, who was a teacher, spoke to me of the dangers of wrongdoing. To make use of the fresh experience, he not only pointed to the prisoners as examples but also, to my surprise, the guards.

'See those *nak tot* (prisoners)? They are as good as dead. Nobody wants anything to do with them even after they are released. That's why we have the word *ki kuk* (jailbird). *Luk* (child), don't ever end up like them.'

'What about the *phu khum* (guards)? They look smart in their uniforms.'

'Those brutes? They aren't much better—former mediocre students who ended up with such jobs because they are qualified for little else. Think about it. Nobody in his right mind would want to work among bad people or mind a tower in hot weather. People fear yet despise them for their violence.'

He paused, as if to wait for my young brain to process what he had just said, before he continued, 'Listen up, if you want to work in a nice office, you had better make good grades from now on.'

Sadly, in my teenage years, I didn't follow his advice and I abandoned my textbooks for my guitar and what I perceived to be the exciting life of a musician. I ventured into the provinces where the American soldiers were stationed during the Vietnam War to play for them and live my dream. Even though I didn't make it as a musician —and my father wouldn't like me saying this—it was worth it.

Por had little regard for either the guards or the inmates. Many years later, however, I saw that guards are prisoners too, given that they spent long hours in a depressing workplace. Some wind down every evening by pouring copious amounts of alcohol down their throats or engaging in other counter-productive activities. At the same time, those same low-paid officials are tempted every day to do deals with the inmates to make some extra cash. Those who succumb to temptation and help to smuggle drugs into the facility, however, are handed twice the usual sentence if they are caught. If there is any honest but dirty job in the world that can really test or taint your spirit, this is it.

The irony is that the guards are called *nai* (master) by the prisoners but by society outside they are viewed as brutes, as my father put it. This reputation exists with good reason. Some guards, especially in the old days, physically abused prisoners or commanded the trustees to do so. (Trustees are prisoners who help the guards to maintain order.) In the past, there was no pressure from human rights groups.

I don't know if this is unique to Thailand but, over the years, I have been the victim of prejudice simply because dealing with inmates is part of my job. That is why I made it my personal mission to use the media exposure I have had as 'Thailand's last executioner' to change the stereotype of the prison guard.

On a larger scale, the stigma and superstitions attached to jails and everyone involved with them is alive and well in Thai society today. Thais still say you are doing something beneath yourself if you work with no-good prisoners. An actor who has to do a scene in a cell will walk into it backwards so as not to end up there in real life.

In the old days, people said that those who went into a prison to visit inmates or to do other business besides serving time would never end up as convicts. They also believed, however, that the prisoners dabbled in black magic. So, in order to counteract the power the prisoners possessed, they would bury unholy items such as broken *bat* (the lidded bowls Buddhist monks use to collect offerings during morning alms) under the main gates of the prisons.

Prisons remain an almost unholy topic and one that we Thais rarely discuss. It has never been an issue that could make or break an election campaign, hence the inadequate funding for the maintenance and development of prisons.

Although I ended up on the better end of the prison system, my late father would not have been too happy about my choice of occupation. Even now, I can only wonder if I was somehow destined to work in prison, as a cousin and my own brother also worked as prison guards for most of their lives. Were the weekend trips to Nonthaburi my prelude to a lifelong career in Bang Kwang? An astrologer once told me that my fate was to work with death. His prediction came true and I have spent 20 years as an executioner.

If there is one thing I have learnt in all these years, it is that life doesn't care what your plan is, if you have any. I believe there are influences that are not under our control that shape the course of our lives. So, at times, I feel life is just a series of random occurrences. Whatever you do, however, you should lead your life with honesty. I would like to believe then things will turn out fine for you. Just don't expect the outcome to be exactly as you had hoped. Roll with it and make the most of what you have.

I was very disheartened indeed when I realised I couldn't continue to play music for a living as I had done. The bars closed at an alarming rate after the American soldiers had left. So I chose what I saw as the best way at that time to provide for my young family: becoming a prison guard. It was not my first choice. In fact, I disliked the civil service ranking system and the practice of pandering to the boss, which is prevalent. But I guess I have learnt to ignore them.

How well the prisons and their inmates are managed in any country says a lot about how highly it values its citizens, good and bad. A developed and humane society will have a system that reflects that.

It also shows how developed the country is in general, I believe. It is a contradiction in terms to purport to be civilised while carrying out the death penalty in any form. So I often find myself asking questions about Thailand.

I cannot dispel entirely the idea of having execution enshrined in law, however, even if it is there just as a warning. The government should make serious efforts to educate the citizens about the existence of such a law and its consequences. The Thai government still has a lot of work to do to in this respect.

Of course, I don't want my children or other students to dwell on the negativity of life but I just can't help but warn them. That's because I've heard too many stories of people who got into trouble or were arrested under the most unlikely circumstances.

I have had my eyes and ears opened to the types of happenings most people don't encounter in their daily lives. It would be a waste if I kept them to myself. Why not let these young minds know what lies ahead?

I may have inherited this tendency towards teaching from my father; my own children told me I could be preachy sometimes when recounting tales.

As I worked in Bang Kwang for more than 30 years, I suppose this gives me the right to share my humble opinion and observations with outsiders. I believe that beneath the gruesome stories, harsh truths and myths, are lessons we all could share.

As my retirement neared, my conviction grew stronger that these stories should be heard. I would like to think I completed this book to the best of my knowledge and with utmost honesty. I feel my voice and those of the people I speak about are significant in painting a complete picture of the Bangkok Hilton: prisoner advocates, former inmates and executed convicts, to name but few.

If any good comes out of this book, I would like to dedicate to those who have contributed to its making, and to the 55 lives I have taken with a machine gun.

Chapter 1 ❧

THE LAST EXECUTIONER

In Thailand, many people call me 'the last executioner'. That is because in the 20 years I spent in that role, I pulled the trigger more often than any of my colleagues, shooting 55 people dead. With the sub machine gun firmly in my hands, I fully acknowledged the human beings before me whose lives I was about to take. Although there was a cloth screen between us offering me some ease, the bullets I fired ruptured the hearts of those who had been condemned to death.

Today capital punishment is carried out by lethal injection in Thailand. Three executioners send deadly chemicals from another room through a tube connected to the arm of a strapped-down convict. Some Thais consider this method not enough of a deterrent, however, as the condemned person does not suffer real pain. The executioners are viewed as administrators of a medical procedure instead of as fearful figures. That was not the case when I was the executioner.

You could say that I had no one to blame but myself for landing this unpleasant title. My first job at Bang Kwang was as a prison guard. Later I became a death row prisoner escort, then the gun adjuster and, finally, the executioner.

I eagerly accepted the chance to be part of the execution team, to show my superiors that I could carry out undesirable tasks and be a valued staff member. Perhaps I could have refused to do it but somebody had to and it happened to be me. I took it as a job and my intention was pure: to carry out court orders and not to take pleasure in killing anybody. Besides, I didn't want to risk offending my superiors by refusing their requests. When each new warden asked me to carry out this task, I did not refuse as he might take it personally, because I had obliged the wardens that went before him.

On the day of an execution, I would go home earlier than usual for a short rest and to get ready. Tew, my wife, picked up on this pattern but usually my silence spoke volumes and she went about the household chores. Later, she would ask resignedly, 'You did one today?'

The execution order had to be carried out confidentially so I never discussed it with her. She could read about it in the next day's newspaper anyway.

For years, she hoped I would give up this extra, undesirable job. She was concerned about my karmic wellbeing as well as my aging body. So after capital punishment by lethal injection was introduced, she dragged me to do merit-making rituals at various temples, buying cows to save from slaughterhouses, and also urged me to be ordained a monk, which I did.

In Buddhism, to take a life is a sin. And yes, I have sinned. However, given my pure intention, I hope karma will be kinder to me. I guess, if you look at it from a different angle, you could say that I helped to speed up karma's work.

In later years, I caught myself sighing deeply with pity, increasingly feeling sorry for those whose lives I was about to cut short. Some of them wailed, pleaded or protested their innocence loudly until the very last minutes of their lives. Others walked to their deaths calmly or even boasted about the number of people they had killed as they were tied to the cross with their backs towards me.

I remember how one man, named Daengyik, begged us for a little more time even as we tied him down to be shot.

'Please, please wait. My mother is talking with the bigwigs. She knows people in the government. She'll come to help me. *Mae* (mother) please help me! I don't want to die,' he said.

His pathetic cries stuck in my mind because they made me wonder whether a condemned person outside Thailand would say something like that. It showed how common the practice of pulling strings is in this country. Making use of contacts can get you a job, a place at a prestigious school or the chance to have your life spared —regardless of whether you deserve it or not.

His pleas fell on deaf ears. Had I not known of his crimes, I might have felt sorry for this grown man who was reduced to crying like a baby. Daengyik's three-man gang of pick-pockets had committed shocking crimes, however, and the military government had ordered summary execution.

They were arrested after one gang member killed a man who had alerted an unsuspecting female that they were trying to steal from her shoulder bag as they all rode a public bus. Enraged, two members of the gang, though not Daengyik, attacked him. One of the thieves grabbed him by his collar while the other stabbed him in the heart in front of the petrified passengers. The gang of three fled unhampered.

Two months earlier, they had also been accused of killing a man in similar circumstances. That man had warned them in parental tones, 'Brothers, you can't do that (picking pockets).' They dragged him off the bus, beat him senseless and stabbed him to death as he tried to run away from them on the streets of Bangkok.

The three men were executed on the same day. Daengyik's mother came to collect her son's body the following day. Despite his wickedness, he was still a person to his mother and his existence meant something to her—though the rest of society wished him nothing but a painful death.

Often when we talk about those who are sentenced to death we focus on the sordid details of their crimes but that won't give you any insight into the minds of these individuals or make you relate to them as people. I would like to share with you some last words from a number of the condemned in the hope of showing you a new way to look at them. I have refrained from using their real names and have also taken the liberty of editing their messages for clarity.

My dear son,

By the time you read this letter, my life will already have been terminated. But before I depart from this world, please do not feel sorry for this disgraceful end to my life. I had no intention to commit the crime I was somehow found guilty of. I didn't sell 'ya ba' (crazy drug or amphetamine). My only crime was borrowing someone else's truck, not knowing what was in it. When you are big, please use my life as a lesson.

I love you, son. Everything I've done, I've done with your best interests in my mind. I'm not the kind of person who breaks the law. You're my son and I worry that the karma I've done in my current and previous lives will somehow haunt you in one way or another. Please be a good boy. I want you to wai [perform the traditional greeting] and ask for forgiveness on my behalf from those whom I caused trouble, including your mother. Everything that happened is all in the past now. Forget them if you can because the hardest part is now over for you. Please focus on your present and, if you concentrate and do your best today, then your future will become good in the long run.

I have to say goodbye now. What good merit I've made so far, I would like to see them reward you, not me. Birth, aging, illness and death are common steps in the cycle of life, like Buddha said. Everyone has to face them sooner or later. Don't feel sorry about my passing.

I want you to know I never harmed anyone and I didn't commit the crime I was found guilty of. I was sentenced to die anyway and you should realise that khon jon *(poor people) in this country can be thrown into prison and executed with no way to protest their innocence because we don't have the resources to do so.*

Take your education seriously and obey your mother. You don't need to come and collect my body. Just come to collect my ashes. (I assume he expressed his intention to be cremated right after the execution instead of running the risk of having his family see his wounded body)

Por

The author of the above letter has stayed in my mind because I too am a father. His thoughts turned to the wellbeing of his child even during the last minutes of his life. He, and the following author maintained their innocence until the end.

To my dearest three friends with respect,

Please take my leave. I wish I could wai *my father at his feet one more time. Please continue to fight for my innocence if you could. I didn't commit the crime they said I did in the verdict. I suffered in this prison for eight years while trying to fight for my innocence to no avail. My lawyer didn't submit documents for my appeal so I didn't get the chance to fight my case through the three courts. I'm so distraught that I haven't been given justice by the authorities. You can ask the lawyer for every detail regarding my case.*

I never have taken a man's life but somehow my life was destined to have a tragic ending. I humbly beg you to continue fighting for my innocence. My children are still young and my wife has taken a new man. I don't know the exact details of who is currently taking care of my children. Please take time to check up on their wellbeing. I last heard that they are being taken care of by a couple living at (the address).

Finally I would like to wai *at the feet of so many people to whom I am indebted with favours they have done for me, including you three.*

On the other hand, there were those who were resigned to their fate and buckled under the weight of their guilt. They accepted the consequences of their own actions for the last time before their lives would be terminated. I've selected two of them to be shown below.

Dear Por, who I most respect,

I'm so glad to have been born as your son, though I will regret eternally not having repaid you enough for what you have done for me. I was prevented from doing so by the consequences of my own action. It's time karma made me repay my wrongdoings with my life and I'm willing to do so. I don't want you or my brother to feel sorry for me or to waste your time mourning my death. Sooner or later, everyone has to die.

Throughout my life, you and my brother are the ones who really cared for me. Brother, please take care of our father after I'm gone. Don't let him down like I did. Support him. Don't sell the family's rice paddy. Work on it and make a living out of it but never sell it. I want to thank everyone from our village too who has offered me kindness and sympathy. Please tell them not to think too much about my departure.

I prostrate myself at your feet, my father and mother.

Father and mother, please take my humble leave. I've committed so few good deeds that my current life has been cut short like this.

[It's conventional belief that if someone dies prematurely it is because they have run out of good karma in this life.]

If there really is reincarnation, I wish my fate would be bound with yours so I could be reborn as your child again. In this life, I've done nothing to make you two proud of me. I only brought troubles and heartache to you. Please forgive me.

I've not done my biggest duty as a son by becoming a monk to make merit on behalf of you two and, for that, I feel terribly sorry. My wish is that I can do that for you in my next life, if it is possible. Sister, please take your education seriously as it will play a big part in how your future turns out and how many choices you will have in life. Mother and father, please take care of yourselves. For whatever I did in the past, please forgive me. I don't have anything else to say.

It's common for the authors of these letters to open their hearts to their loved ones and I admit that some of these messages were touching. They showed that, regardless of what they had done wrong, they were still human and their existence meant something to somebody. However, sympathy mustn't excuse them for their crimes.

I didn't read any of these last letters or the cases before the executions. It was my rule not to research the execution cases until they were over in order to prevent myself from investing any emotion in pulling the trigger. I didn't want to run the risk of taking pleasure in executing certain convicts, whom I later found to be very contemptible. That would make me no better than a murderer. On the other hand, I couldn't shoot someone if I doubted their guilt, so the best policy was to know nothing regarding the circumstances of the person before me.

It is impossible for those of us who are free to understand the feelings of a condemned man or woman but I used to hope that they tried to think of good deeds they had done in their lives. We Thais believe the state of mind in which we leave the earth greatly influences our wellbeing in the afterlife. So if you think positively, you are likely to have a better status in this world when you come back. I know it sounds absurd for them to think of anything else besides the pain they were about to experience but I genuinely thought this belief would help them.

When I was a prisoner escort, I used to explain this idea to those I collected from their cells in the hope that it would calm their minds. It is ironic that such advice came from a messenger of death. What a petty gesture of kindness I gave them just minutes before their demise.

Later, with each execution I performed, I would ask the convicts for forgiveness in my mind and then empty it of negative feelings in order to focus on the duty at hand. I looked to my right to a flag-holding officer to signal to him that I was ready. He lowered the red flag and I sent bullets through the bull's eye that was placed on the cloth screen to help me take aim. In the blink of an eye, they pierced the heart of the condemned person. A small pool of blood started to form at the base of the cross and some blood splattered onto the sandbags in front of them. The sound of the machine gun, though muffled by a silencer, was amplified as the room fell silent for few moments. Brief croaking sounds ensued as their spirits slowly and painfully departed from bodies.

They were untied from the cross and put in a room awaiting collection by their relatives the following day. The more fortunate were buried quietly or cremated while the less fortunate ones were simply left there. Their relatives held them in contempt because they had tainted the family name and they decided to humiliate them, even in their death. In such cases, Bang Kwang Central Prison cremates the remains in co-operation with the adjoining Buddhist temple.

When I was a guide at the Corrections Museum later, the fact that I had been an executioner seemed to add an extra chill to the tour for some visitors. As I explained how the equipment was once used on actual human beings in order to test their innocence, their faces registered disbelief and terror.

The museum houses equipment for use in torture, restraint, punishment and execution dating back to Ayutthaya era, which ran from 1350 to 1767. There is also prison memorabilia such as the handmade drug-taking apparatus used by prisoners. It was opened in 1939 and, after a few relocations, is now in part of the building that used to be the Bangkok Remand Prison on Mahachai Road.

As a guide, I felt it was my responsibility to be able to answer questions the visitors had that were beyond the exhibits themselves. So I did extensive study of the history of Thailand's prisons and judicial system. It helped me to understand the stories behind many of the strange items on display.

The main exhibition building houses paintings depicting gruesome ancient forms of punishment such as being caged and eaten alive by starved dogs, being burnt alive or being tied to a cross and having one's skull opened while still alive. These were reserved for those who had committed severe crimes. Three types of whips were used, one of which was said to be soaked in salt water to ensure excruciating pain was inflicted.

One tactic used to obtain confessions involved making the accused lie down in a small coffin with his hands tied. There were two small air holes in the lid to ensure that the person inside suffered greatly but did not suffocate. To make matters worse, the box was placed under the glaring sun.

One piece that seems to draw the attention of Thai and foreign visitors alike is a rattan ball called *takro*. A convict would be made to enter this 80cm diameter ball and assume the foetal position. The ball would then be kicked around by an elephant as the man inside was cut and stabbed by sharp nails sticking into the ball's interior.

Another horrifying centrepiece is a hook called *bet lek*. It looks like a T on a tripod standing slightly taller than a grown man. The T, with a central pivot, has arms that can tilt in the same way a balance does with a pulley and a hook on one arm. The offender was made to stand with his hands tied behind his back while the hook pierced his chin from beneath. The punisher then pulled the rope to gradually lift the hook, leaving the offender with no choice but to stand on his toes while it further dug into the inside of his mouth.

Looking past the disturbing nature of these exhibits, you will see the progress of civilisations. Torture used to be part of ancient judicial proceedings but societies have abandoned such practices in order to adopt a fairer, more humane approach to punishment.

Chapter 2 ❧

ANCIENT JUSTICE

C ontrary to what you might expect, however, trial by ordeal and barbaric penalties were not the norm at the dawn of Thai civilization in the Sukhothai era, which ran from 1238 to about 1350.

At that time, King Ramkhamhaeng the Great, the third monarch of the first kingdom, who is credited as the inventor of the Thai language, allowed his subjects to ring a bell placed at the front of his palace if they wished to have an audience. He would then listen to their complaints and settle disputes between his subjects in person. This shows how close the benevolent king was to his subjects.

To avoid the threat of an epidemic, King U Thong, the founding king of Thailand's second kingdom, moved his court to establish a new capital named Ayutthaya in 1350. He succeeded in peacefully taking Sukhothai as a part of his kingdom as a tributary state and declared Theravada Buddhism as the national religion. King U

Thong introduced a law based on the Hindu code of conduct called Dharmashastra to govern his kingdom.

Subsequent kings of Ayutthaya supplemented the Thai legal system by introducing other laws to cover a wide range of human activities as the society became more complex throughout more than 400 years of the kingdom. Ayutthayan laws remained in force until the late 19th century when legal reformation took place in the reign of King Chulalongkorn.

Under ancient law, judicial procedures involved physical torture. This practice was known as *Jareet Nakhonban* and the accused would be subjected to torture for crimes they were presumed to have committed. It is likely that innocent people confessed to the bogus accusations levelled against them out of fear of pain and death.

If they could bring a witness to testify in their favour, however, they might be found innocent. In other words, the defendants had to act as their own attorneys and prove the accusations were unfounded.

Besides the use of violence during criminal proceedings, I have read many strange accounts of what was lawfully acceptable then. For example, it was legal for parents to assault a man who had sneaked into their house to meet their daughter without their consent. Householders could stab burglars who had broken into their homes. A charge could be brought against those who merely behaved suspiciously. Neighbours would be punished if they themselves couldn't catch the thieves. This was deemed justified as necessary to keep the peace in the community as it would discourage neighbours from providing a hiding place to thieves. There was no such thing as '*in dubio pro reo*,' when in doubt, favour the accused, or 'innocent until proven guilty'.

The living conditions of prisoners were deplorable. In *Du Royaume de Siam*, French ambassador Simon de La Loubère described prisoners being confined in cages or pens made of bamboo while completely at the mercy of all kinds of weather. He visited Siam (as Thailand was known until 1939) in 1687 during the reign of Narai the Great, a king who was known for his foreign diplomacy.

The Frenchman also wrote that trial by ordeal took place in front of an audience. The plaintiff and defendant were subjected to various tests to prove their innocence. Those who showed a higher pain threshold and suffered less physical damage than others were deemed to be telling the truth. For instance, the one whose heel didn't swell after walking through fire or whose hands were less damaged after putting them into boiling oil would be the righteous one. Likewise the one who could hold their breath underwater longer was the one who spoke the truth, it was reasoned, because divine intervention would be at work protecting the virtuous.

In a milder test, each of the litigants would be given vomit-inducing medicine and subjected to curses by Buddhist monks. The person who didn't vomit would be named as the honest one. In the event that both litigants were harmed or both were unharmed, they would have to undergo another test.

Another account described eight prisons holding men convicted of *dacoity* (robbery) each with a cell for their respective wives and children in front of them. Ten *dacoits* (robbers) who had received more lenient sentences would be grouped as one with a neck chain and taken out to do public work. Those who had received harsher sentences would also be tied together using a neck chain but in groups ranging from twenty to thirty. On Buddhist holy days, these prisoners were sent out to markets to beg for food along with their wives and children, each of whom had two fetters (presumably around their ankles and wrists). They were joined together with a rope tied around their waists. This showed that for some offences the wrongdoers and their families were punished.

The ancient system, flawed as it was, did have a way to prevent corruption and the miscarriage of justice, to an extent. It is said that if a litigant believed his judge had received a bribe or was colluding with his legal opponent to facilitate an unfavourable verdict, he could petition the royal court or a nobleman of a rank higher than that of the nobleman who had acted as his first judge. The first judge would then become the defendant to the petitioner.

However, this kind of appeal was not done to reverse the given verdict but to punish corrupt judges, as no legal contest on the same dispute between the litigants would be allowed in a higher court. The judge who was found guilty as charged would have to pay a fine and a court fee for the appellant, and vice versa. In theory, the petition process could be repeated many times up the administrative hierarchy line until the case reached the kings' ears. In reality, petitioners would give up the fight for fear that their action would result in retaliation from the judges.

The Ayutthaya era lasted until 1767 when the capital was brought to ruin by the Burmese army. Siam was in chaos until it was reestablished by King Taksin, a military commander born to a Chinese father and a Thai mother, who chose Thonburi, situated across the Chao Phraya River from Bangkok, to be the new capital. He was later declared mentally unstable, supposedly as a result of the toll taken on his mind by being constantly at war. In a rebellion led by Phraya San, King Taksin was deposed and forced to become a monk.

When General Chao Phraya Chakri heard of the instability in the capital while he was on a campaign against Cambodia, he returned to Thonburi to put down the rebellion. The general, who later became King Rama I and the founder of the current ruling Chakri dynasty, ordered an investigation, punished the rebels and, to prevent further chaos, ordered that King Taksin be executed.

There are a few possibilities as to how King Taksin's reign came to a tragic end. One account revealed he was put in velvet bag and beaten to death with a scented sandalwood club in April 1782. Another account claimed that a stand-in was beaten to death in his place and he was sent to live in the Nakhon Si Thammarat province in the south of Thailand. Thai people still discuss the circumstances surrounding the demise of his 15-year reign.

The end of Thonburi ushered in the current era of Thailand, which is called Rattanakosin, and the kings of Chakri dynasty have ruled Thailand ever since.

At first the current kingdom adopted the same law codes used in Ayutthaya, although many were lost when the former capital was destroyed. The revision and collection of ancient laws took place following an unusual verdict. A man called Boonsri petitioned against the judge Phra Kasem for being unfair by awarding a divorce to his wife Amdaeng Pom, who had committed adultery with a man named Racha-at. However, the ancient law stipulated that a 'woman who requests to be separated from her blameless man should be allowed to do so'. King Rama I expressed his concern that the ancient laws had become irrelevant and ordered them to be revised.

The real turning point for the Thai legal system came about as a result of Siam opening up to trade with western countries and facing the threat of colonisation in the 19th century. Great Britain was the first to demand extraterritoriality, which would make its subjects exempt from local laws, the reduction of import duties to three percent and the abolition of the Thai Royal Treasury's monopoly of foreign trade as stated in the Bowring Treaty, signed in 1855 by King Rama IV or King Mongkut and Sir John Bowring, the fourth governor of Hong Kong.

Despite its official title as the Treaty of Friendship and Commerce, it could be seen as an unfair contract given that Britain had already demonstrated its military might during the First Opium War with the Qing Dynasty of China from 1839 to 1842. That war forced China to allow free trade in certain ports. Siam feared it was in no position to negotiate either.

In addition, five years before the Bowring Treaty, failed negotiations between King Rama III and Sir James Brooke, the White Rajah of Sarawak and British envoy, had served to heighten tensions. At that time, Brooke's attempts to negotiate for more freedom of trade and exemption from Siamese laws for British subjects had come to nothing. This resulted in his advising that force be used to make Siam more open to foreign trade.

Before his passing, King Rama III reportedly stated that Siamese warfare with Burma or Yuan (Vietnam) would be no more but that the new threat came from westerners. 'We should study their innovations for our own benefit but not to the degree of obsession or worshipping them,' he said.

His parting words coincided with the subsequent capitulation of Burma and Vietnam to colonial rule by the British and the French, respectively.

After the Bowring Treaty, the next 13 bilateral treaties between Siam and western countries each imposed extraterritoriality as a condition. Under these agreements, disputes between Siamese and foreign subjects would be determined by the consul of their respective countries in amicable conjunction with Siamese officers. Foreign offenders were subject to their laws and Siamese offenders to Thai law. The consuls wouldn't interfere in matters solely concerned with the Siamese, nor would the Siamese authorities interfere in questions that concerned only foreign subjects.

Back then, Siam had courts under each ministry though they were not the exact equivalent of their western counterparts, especially as trial by ordeal was still used. These courts were unique, questioning the defendant and acting as the judge.

Officials involved in the legal process could be divided into two groups. One group, called *luk khun*, specialised in law codes. The other group was made up of officials who either were involved in the court hearing or carried out specific duties as part of the legal proceedings.

A legal action began when a private accuser brought a complaint against someone. An accuser had to see an official who would write down his complaint. The official then passed it on to another official who would send the case to the *luk khun*, who then would decide if it had merit or not.

The accuser ran the risk of being punished if his complaint was found to be frivolous. If not, the nature of case would be assessed and it would be assigned to a court under a ministry deemed suitable to process it. The testimony would then be sent to the *luk khun* who decided whether the defendant or the plaintiff should lose the case or if it needed further investigation. The verdict was then sent to another official who gauged what kind of punishment would be handed down before the judge carried out the punishment. Besides having their own courts, many ministries also had their own jails.

During the reign of King Chulalongkorn, Siam reformed various aspects of its legal systems and abolished slavery, in order to appear as a civilised country and to avert colonisation.

His Majesty, the fifth king of the Chakri dynasty, managed to keep the country independent even as France and Britain controlled most of Southeast Asia. However, Siamese autonomy came with a price. Some of its territories, namely parts of what are now Laos, Cambodia and northern Malaysia, were handed to these two powers to save the majority of the country.

Prince Rabi, the 'father of modern Thai law' and King Chulalongkorn's son, noted at the time that Siam's legal system was ineffective. He wrote: 'Under old criminal proceedings, those who faced criminal charges would suffer greatly. They would be detained before a court hearing could take place which took a long time, unlike today. Moreover, during a hearing, the accused was presumably viewed as a criminal. Court officials tended to hit or whip the accused to obtain evidence. If the accused could find a witness to testify of his innocence, he could be acquitted. In other words, the accused himself had to prove the charge levied against him was bogus. Today the accused is viewed as innocent until proven guilty.'

About trial by ordeal, he said, 'It was open to abuse by the judges, resulting in people losing respect for them and seeing them as demons.' He pointed out that the judges didn't exercise any lenience because low-ranking

ANCIENT JUSTICE

judges were under pressure to perform and answer to their superiors.

Prince Rabi exposed another glaring flaw in the system of old, that of limitless imprisonment. Under the old law, imprisonment was for life—unless the king graciously pardoned the convicts or reduced the term of the sentence. 'The courts always bring petitions seeking clemency from the king. His Majesty is always diligent to commute a period of imprisonment case by case for criminals from all over the country. However, such a task is simply too overwhelming to be carried out alone.'

Many prisoners were imprisoned for years without proper cause or judgment. In an 1891 letter to King Rama V, the chief prison doctor wrote that he had met a patient who had been imprisoned for 28 years for a petty offence and, on top of this, he had yet to be told whether he had been found guilty. Another account said a man named Ai Rung had been imprisoned for gang robbery along with nine other men. After 14 years, only Ai Rung survived, though he still did not know either what offence he was supposed to have committed or the limit of his sentence.

An 1890 account by Prince Damrong Rajanupab, King Mongkut's son, told of a case of royal pardon. At a meeting, King Rama V told those present that he had received a rather unusual petition letter from a prisoner named Ai Tim from Intaburi town. Ai Tim had been incarcerated for 10 years for robbery. In the letter, he said that throughout his imprisonment, he had been trained in the craft of making rattan wares. He had made it his mission to create a masterpiece in the hope of giving it to His Majesty. Should King Chulalongkorn be pleased with his work, he would beg His Majesty to kindly grant him a pardon. Ai Tim said, if freed, he intended to be a monk for the rest of his life and never return to his old ways. At the end of his letter, he vowed that if his message contained any false information, he would be willing to receive capital punishment from His Majesty.

Not every prisoner would be granted a pardon if his petition reached the king; any good deeds performed and the time served in jail would be taken into consideration as well. Ten years in jail made Ai Tim eligible for consideration for a royal pardon. After verifying Ai Tim's words, at the next meeting, His Majesty was presented with one of his pieces of rattan handicraft. His Majesty took a look at the meticulous work and said, 'He spoke the truth. I shall make him see the result of being truthful.'

Ai Tim was released and ordained at the Wat Pho temple in Bangkok. In 1893, at the time of a dispute between France and Siam, Phra (monk) Tim expressed his intention to leave the temple in order to volunteer to fight against the French to repay His Majesty's kindness. He said when he was young he had learnt some magic that could be useful against the French and, if he survived the war, he would resume his monastic life.

His Majesty was pleased to hear of Ai Tim's offer but turned him down and told him to continue his monastic life instead, as he was too old for warfare. Ai Tim returned to his temple and died several years later as a monk.

In 1896, King Chulalongkorn granted the metropolitan court and provincial courts the power to put limits on sentences. He also entrusted Prince Rabi to work on older cases where a prison term had yet to be specified.

In terms of prison management, King Chulalongkorn assigned an official to survey prisons and hospitals in Singapore, which was a British colony at the time. This led to the construction of the Kong Mahantatot Prison on Mahachai Road in Bangkok by a British contractor. This was the first modern prison. It had a kitchen, four buildings for holding prisoners and seven towers on its walls. The prisoners were transferred to this new prison on 28 July 1891 after ten Buddhist monks had chanted blessings, performed rituals and thrown holy water and sand around the walls to ward off any illnesses.

Overcrowding was a problem, as mentioned by Momchao Sa-nga Ngam (Momchao is a title given to a king's grandchild) in a report on a prison named Taranglahutot, in Bangkok, dated April 29, 1893. At that time, the prison held inmates who had been sentenced to less than six months and those awaiting trial. It had seventeen cells for male and female inmates. Two of them held 205 female inmates in total while the rest were supposedly built to hold 120 men each, though there were 2,019 male inmates in total. This means the number of the male inmates exceeded the prison's capacity by 219 and more were being sent from the courts. Some prisoners were asked to sleep on the brick floors in the halls in front of their cells.

Overcrowding remains a problem in Thai prisons. The Bangkok Hilton holds the record, as it once housed almost 8,000 inmates when its actual capacity was half that number. In recent years, the inmates have been sent out to other major prisons to reduce overcrowding.

King Chulalongkorn declared that as the country had become increasingly progressive, the unsightly prisons should be located outside Bangkok. So a large plot of land on the east side of the Chao Phraya River in Nonthaburi province was purchased with the intention of building a new facility. A law school and the city hall of Nonthaburi were built on the land later, however, leaving not enough space for a prison.

After additional land had been purchased, in the reign of King Rama VII, the first phase of the construction of what was later dubbed the Bangkok Hilton began in 1927, with the aim of establishing Thailand's first maximum-security prison.

A Frenchman named Charles was the architect of this project. His design was based on European and American prisons and includes a 30-metre-high tower that allows guards to oversee all activities on the prison grounds. Four years later, in July 1931, prisoners from Kong Mahantatot in Bangkok were transferred to this new prison.

Originally Bang Kwang was for prisoners sentenced to more than 10 years in jail or to death. Now it holds prisoners sentenced to more than thirty years in jail from every corner of the country. It has long been notorious for holding the worst offenders in Thailand.

Chapter 3 ❧

INTRODUCING LETHAL INJECTIONS

One of earliest accounts of capital punishment appears in an Ayutthayan law code issued in 1435. It lists the 21 horrific forms of death penalty handed down to the perpetrators of such serious crimes as rebellion, killing of monks or teachers, parenticide, vandalising of images of Buddha, abducting and dismembering an infant in order to remove accessories from its body. These included being eaten alive by starving dogs, getting cut to death little by little, having heated metal dropped onto their exposed brains, or having their skin peeled off from neck to waist in vertical strips that were left to drape over the lower halves of their bodies. Given the unfathomable amount of pain, it is highly unlikely that anyone could survive these barbaric retributions.

Following a homicide, the convict would be brought before the head of the victim's family, who had a say in whether he should be killed or not, though the authority to order capital punishment belonged to the king alone. Sometimes, the victim's family forgave the murderer and asked him to become a monk for the rest of his life to make merit on behalf of the dead person.

In 1908, decapitation by sword was officially declared the only form of capital punishment acceptable under Thai law. It usually took place within the holy precincts of a Buddhist monastery in front of an audience. The public beheading served to discourage others from wrongdoing. Some accounts say cemeteries were used as execution venues too.

The beheadings involved a series of steps, all with their own rituals and superstition. It also required special equipment. At that time, the shackles put on convicts' legs had no locks. So a postmortem knife, which was like a butcher's knife, was used specifically to cut the heels off the feet of the headless corpses so the irons could be removed. This knife became obsolete after removable shackles were introduced in 1894. A second knife, called *mitmo* (sorcerer's magic knife), was believed to be infused with occult power. It was used solely to cut the yarn that designated the area reserved for the execution.

There are three known types of execution sword. They were made by the execution master, who decided which one to use on a case by case basis.

A wooden cross was fixed firmly into the ground. The master executioner made a hole in the ground, called Phra Mae Thorani (earth personified as female deity) next to it and asked from her forgiveness for the transgression that was about to transpire—spilling blood over her. The master then wrote in occult script on the ground at the cross, marking the spot where the convict would sit, and placed a banana leaf over it.

The convict sat with his back to the cross and his legs extended forward. He was secured there with white string. He put his hands together in the prayer position with flowers between his palms. Mud was used to cover his ears and mouth, and to mark the spot on his neck where the sword would cut through.

Before and after every beheading, the executioner's team sprinkled their bodies with holy water to repel angry spirits of decapitated convicts who might try to harm or possess them. Red flags were stuck in the ground to mark the execution area and those who weren't involved in the act weren't allowed to enter. Convicts would be taken out of the prison in the early hours of the morning and transferred to the execution venue by boat.

A makeshift altar, which looked like a split-level table, was erected. The higher level was for the offerings and the lower level was for the swords and knives. A big ornate brass tray, for example, was filled such offerings as a pig's head and a fish. The master executioner performed a ritual to pay his respects to the spirits and higher beings, inviting them all to preside over the proceedings. Then the primary and secondary executioners joined him in more rituals. The master then anointed them with sacred flour on their foreheads before handing them the blessed swords. The executioners paid their respects to their teachers and deities they held in high regard, to gain moral support before proceeding. The convict was then offered his last meal.

The executioners wore special red outfits, which were designed to conform with superstition. Their uniforms consisted of a vest, a waist sash, knee-length shorts and a garland of yarn for the head. Occult symbols on these items were believed to imbue them with power. They served the same purpose as holy water: protecting the executioners from the vengeful spirits of the beheaded.

Branches were gathered to make an arch called *pratu pee* (ghost door), which served as entrance to and exit from the site of the decapitation for the executioners. It was destroyed immediately afterwards to prevent the spirits of the decapitated from returning to their homes or following the executioners to harm.

Before the beheading, the team would stay within a sacred circle marked with white yarn called *saisin*. The primary executioner put holy water in a big bowl behind the condemned while the secondary executioner sat in front. A band played the flute and drums as they began. The primary executioner performed the highest form of respect, as if the king were presiding over the proceedings.

The executioner then lifted his sword and moved slowly towards the convict. It was said that then he would stamp on the ground but, if the sound startled the convict, he would lower his weapon and wait. He would strike only when his stomp received no response.

The initial cut would not be enough to sever the head cleanly, however. So immediately afterwards, the first executioner rushed off to wash his face with holy water in the holy circle. Then the secondary executioner finished the job with a second cut and threw the head into the hole the execution team had prepared.

The second executioner then rushed into the holy circle as the first executioner sprinkled him with holy water. The rest of the five-man team, who had been waiting in the holy circle, went out to untie the lifeless body and kick it into the hole.

In some cases, the heads of the condemned would be put on tall sticks and displayed in public for further humiliation and to deter others. Sometimes the bodies of the condemned were cut into pieces and used to feed vultures and crows. Another account states that there were three sword wielders and that the condemned would be whipped 90 times before being beheaded.

The modern legal system had been long introduced in Thailand before Prime Minister Phraya Pahonphonpayuhasena proposed the abolition of capital punishment to the cabinet in 1934. He was the second premier of Thailand after political reform replaced the absolute monarchy with a constitutional monarchy in 1932. His proposal caused widespread debate. Many people did not want capital punishment removed as they feared crime rates would increase.

Eventually it was decided that capital punishment was necessary as a deterrent and the debate shifted to whether to use electrocution or shooting, as decapitation was inhumane.

A lack of proper training meant that sometimes executioners missed the spot on the convict's neck that could deliver sudden death and instead hit the head. These hackings resulted in horrific scenes of convicts painfully struggling between life and death. During their last hours, some convicts buckled under the immense fear of what might happen and they appeared to go insane.

At the time, the government was also concerned at how expensive beheadings were, saying the fees paid to the executioners and the costs involved in performing rituals were too high. Shooting was chosen as it would reduce costs in the long run and eliminate the excessive rituals.

The last person to be decapitated was a man named Boonpheng. His execution took place in 1931. Boonpheng was an orphan who was raised by his maternal grandparents. He grew up to be a charismatic but directionless young man.

Although he seemed to have no aim in life, he was obsessed with sorcery. He studied magic and other superstitious practices with an undertaker at a Buddhist temple. Although he had no real prospects of success, his good looks won him many female admirers.

The kind of magic he was studying usually was intended to produce negative outcomes, so his grandparents tried to discourage him from using it, but to no avail. When their pleas became too much for him, he moved to the Banglampoo area of Bangkok to start his own life. From then on, his reputation as a sorcerer spread quickly as he offered various services from performing a ritual to extend one's life expectancy to making love charms. He attracted a lot of female followers. Some were seen visiting him at night before disappearing. It turned out that he would have sex with his victims before killing them. Then he chopped them into pieces, which he put into metal boxes and then dumped in a canal near his house.

His last victim, a wealthy woman, met her demise in a different manner. Abandoned by her husband, she took comfort in his company and became his regular lover for a while before she fell pregnant with his child. She then demanded that Boonpheng take her as his wife publicly. For this, he decided to kill her.

After murdering her and their unborn child, he went into hiding in Ayutthaya province where he became a monk. Later he resigned from the temple to marry another woman. Before he could become her husband, however, he was arrested and charged with killing seven women. The police had found seven boxes filled with human remains.

His execution was held in public and there were many people there to witness it, though the woman he intended to marry did not show up nor any relatives.

Reportedly, the executioner hacked at his neck with a sword but it didn't get through. The executioner demanded, 'Take off whatever protection you have.' He found an amulet on his body, threw it away and resumed the proceedings. Witnesses said Boonpheng murmured something seconds before his head was severed. They assumed he was chanting magic in an attempt to save his own life but his magic didn't stand a chance against the sword. This time the impact was fatal. His head fell off his shoulders as the audience let out screams. Blood gushed from his torso.

His relatives showed up later to arrange his cremation. It is rumored that his back resisted the fire initially. His ashes were stored in a small stupa at Pasee Temple in Bangkok. A shrine was erected in his name and some people pay respects to him there even now. They believe his spirit remains in this world. It is strange to think that Boonpheng has been elevated from serial killer to an entity worthy of respect.

The first person to be executed by machine gun at Bang Kwang Central Prison was Sawat Mahamad. His execution took place on September 11, 1935, for a crime perpetrated against the royal family.

Opinions vary as to whether capital punishment is necessary or not. The relatives of a killer and those who have never lost a loved one to murder may say they are against the idea but the relatives of the victim may want a life for a life.

One of the main arguments put forward by those in favour of such a penalty in Thailand is that if offenders are treated too leniently, the injured parties could feel aggrieved or even seek to take revenge personally. This reminds me of one case in particular where relatives of both the offender and the victim had a chance to voice their feelings.

In February 1980, nine men gang-raped a young girl called Lumduan and then killed her. One of them was her own relative named Somkid, a police officer. Her mother Wern was distraught and couldn't believe that her own relative could inflict such an unspeakable act on her daughter.

In a newspaper interview, Wern said: 'Honestly, if they would allow me to kill Somkid myself I would not hesitate to do so because I am so angry. And I want to kill them the same way they killed my daughter. My heart ached when I saw the bruises on her body. I want them to suffer the same way my daughter did. Shooting them is too easy. It doesn't offer me an ounce of satisfaction.'

It was quite a statement to hear from a mild-mannered, middle-aged woman dressed in a simple blouse and sarong. The crime shocked the nation and four of the nine men were sentenced to summary execution under the regime of the then military government. Wern worried, however, that the five who had been given lighter sentences would try to harm her later.

On the other hand, Mee, Somkid's adoptive mother, said the death penalty given to her son was justified because of the severity of the crime, though she couldn't believe he could have done such a thing as it was so out of character.

Execution by shooting remained in effect until October 19, 2003, when the then warden of Bang Kwang Central Prison Pittaya Sangkanakin held a press conference to announce that it would be replaced by lethal injection from that day onwards. Four Buddhist monks performed rituals on the two crosses where convicts had been put to death. I was there to hand over to the new team.

I put the HK MP5 submachine gun into its box, looked at it for the last time, before closing the lid and putting a lock it, marking the end of execution by gun. I looked at a plate placed above the entrance of the execution room. It says 'Place to End All Sorrow' though it should be called the 'death chamber'. The ceremony concluded with 319 balloons being set free to symbolise the emancipation of the souls of the condemned from the prison. Three of them were female, six of them were foreigners from Burma, Laos, Taiwan and Hong Kong, and the rest were Thai males. I had pulled the trigger on 55 of them.

After execution by lethal injection was introduced, I decided to enter a monastery for 15 days in November 2003. There were three reasons for my decision. First, it was to fulfil a long overdue duty as a son to my parents. Every Thai man is expected to become a monk at least once in his life as a way to make merit on behalf of his parents and to show how grateful he is to them. I was 55 years old but had been distracted from this duty by the business of raising a family. Second, there was a mass ordination being organised in honour of His Majesty the King on the auspicious occasion of his birthday and the merit the monks made was also devoted to the beloved king. Third, it was my way to make merit for those I had wronged including the people I put to death or helped to put to death.

My wife joked that, of all the men being ordained, I was the one who needed merit-making the most. She was concerned about my spiritual wellbeing. All in all, it is a beautiful tradition and it provided me with a break from the usual business of living. I didn't feel truly comfortable as a monk but I was glad to complete another rite of passage of a Thai man.

Early on the morning of December 12, 2003, eight of my fellow monks, who also had worked as prison guards, and I decided to perform a well-wishing ritual for the souls of executed prisoners at Bang Preak Tai Buddhist Temple, which shares a wall with Bang Kwang. We thought it would be a good idea since we were leaving the temple in few days to resume our jobs at Bang Kwang. Little did we know the first lethal injection in Thailand would be administrated that afternoon.

That day marked a new chapter for the death penalty in Thailand. The Department of Corrections ordered Bang Kwang Central Prison to carry out an order to execute four men. Three of them were drug offenders and the other one had committed premeditated murder. At that time, there were about 6,700 inmates in Bang Kwang, 851 of them on death row and shackled.

A guard on duty that day told to me later what had happened.

'By 3pm, we had already overseen food being given to them and asked them to return to their cells,' he said. 'It was earlier than usual and this made them realise what was about to happen. Many of them lost their appetites. After the last of them was returned to his cell, we locked them in. We closed the main door of the building but didn't lock it and this confirmed to them that at least one of them would walk out that door and never return.

'The usual sound of them chatting and playing around was replaced by silence. About 4pm, the main door opened and revealed 12 prisoner escorts in black vests standing at the doorway. Three escorts per convict [is standard], so, it was four convicts to be put to death that day. I led the escorts to the cells where the four men were to be collected. We made it brisk. Four names were called and they obediently walked out of their cells. Some answered loud and clear showing readiness to "go". Perhaps, they took comfort in knowing that they would suffer less than those who had preceded them.'

The prisoners and their relatives didn't have time to *tham jai* (prepare mentally) before the execution. No one knew it was going to happen as it was kept secret from everyone. Other prisoners on death row have to live with the fear that every day may be their last day.

They were escorted to an office where more officials waited for them and were informed that their petitions for royal pardon from the king had been rejected. They signed their names to acknowledge their respective execution orders. Police from the Criminal Records Division and the prison's records officer verified photographs and fingerprints of the four men before they were allowed to write their wills and letters.

Panom Changthonglek, at 32 the youngest of them, made a long distance phone call to his mother who lived in a southern province. She wasn't home so he left a message with his sister.

'Please tell *Mae* that I'm being executed today,' he said before he put down the phone. Executions are carried out without prior warning to prevent convicts from committing suicide or harming themselves in an attempt to have the execution postponed.

They were offered a big last meal, which included some of the best-known Thai delicacies such as green curry and coconut soup with chicken. They didn't touch the food but asked for water and cigarettes instead. They listened to a last sermon from a monk at the visiting area before being transported on golf cars to a gazebo where they were blindfolded. There they performed rituals to ask for forgiveness.

In the execution room, two of them at a time were asked to lie down on separate beds. A heart rate monitor, showing their vital signs, faced the officers who were there to act as witnesses. Each was restrained at five points—legs, torso and arms—and stabbed with needles in the veins on the backs of both hands. Only one needle was connected to a long tube. The other needle is there in case the first doesn't work. Three executioners were waiting to release three chemicals at the other end of the tubes in a separate room.

Sodium pentothal was sent in first to sedate them. Pancuronium bromide was sent in next to relax their muscles. Potassium chloride was the last to go in to stop their hearts. The cost of the three chemicals used on each of them was only about 200 baht. The prison doctor was there to confirm their deaths and announce the time of death. The executions transpired without a hitch. Their bodies were kept in cold storage at minus 18 Celsius until the next morning when the prison doctor checked to confirm they were dead. Then the corpses were taken to Bang Preak Tai Temple through a small door the guards call the 'ghost door'.

After I retired, I had a feeling that more execution orders would be coming to Bang Kwang because drugs are rife in Thailand. That premonition came true when lethal injections were administered almost six years later to two drug offenders on August 24, 2009. They had been found to be in possession of more than 110,000 amphetamine tablets with intent to sell them. Their assets, which amounted to 73 items worth about 41 million baht, were confiscated.

Although it is well known that the death penalty can be imposed for drug offences here, it seems drug dealers are not deterred. Arrests of major dealers feature regularly on the front pages of Thai newspapers. Some of them have connections with local dealers while some sell their wares to foreigners at tourist islands. They take their chances because they know that if they can get away with it, they will make the type of money could never get from working in honest jobs. No money can make up for a lifetime lost in prison, however.

Drugs have ravaged our society. They destroy the addicts, who commit crimes to get the money to buy more, and those who are close to them. Hallucinating addicts have held innocent people hostage with knives to their throats.

I think the death penalty will be in effect in Thailand for years to come. The notion that the introduction of lethal injection will serve as a stepping stone towards the abolition of death penalty is patently untrue, at least for now.

Chapter 4 ❧

PRISON VISITORS

B ang Kwang prison is not a place for anyone with no real business there. The officials have their hands full as it is a seriously over-crowded and under-resourced facility, holding some of Thailand's most dangerous men. Yet posters on Khao San Road advertising prison visits have made it an alternative 'must-see' destination for many western tourists, particularly young back-packers. It has now become part of the standard itinerary for a lot of visitors to Thailand. I can't help but think that some drop into the prison simply in search of cheap thrills and so they can show their friends at home how adventurous they are by going into the Big Tiger.

Although I have no doubt that most of the western inmates in Bang Kwang appreciate visitors from abroad, the motives behind the visits of these drop-in tourists have to be questioned. Putting it on a tourist map creates problems. It's against regulations to allow drop-in visitors who know the inmates simply from posters. I'm sure no self-respecting guidebook in a western country would include an active high-security prison as an attraction.

In a way, inmates are the forgotten underprivileged people. Many of the Asian prisoners come from poor backgrounds and are cut off by their families when they get into trouble. Foreign inmates are locked away in alien land. On top of that, the prison runs on an inadequate budget, which is why there are many businesses, honest or not, inside.

The conventional thought here is that inmates do not deserve help, and some prison guards assume female visitors are lonely souls who cannot get male attention on the outside and have to look for it in a prison. Yet some Thai people can look past that and give up their time to assist needy convicts. There are also a number of expatriates living in Thailand who visit inmates regularly. They really want to help them and to improve their living conditions and have more than proved themselves to the Thai authorities. The irony is that the much-feared Bang Kwang prison is where I have met the best kind of people as well as the worst.

One group of prison visitors calls itself Jailbird. The founding members were volunteers appointed by the British Embassy in Bangkok and most of them are from the British Women's Group. Although it is not a nice nickname, they don't mind as they jokingly refer to themselves as old birds anyway. One such visitor, Gale Bailey, has become a good friend and we share a mutual love of the Beatles and have been out to see a Beatles tribute band. She is a visitor with single agenda: to help others.

She says: 'It is hard to imagine how one could build friendship with an inmate, isn't it? It took me only one visit and I was hooked. Despite the unpleasant circumstances, we are simply good friends: the chaps, their families and us visitors. I enjoy talking to the chaps as they do to me. There is no mention of age differences nor is there any sexual aspect to our meetings at all. We air our problems to each other and have good laugh together just like friends anywhere do.

'My husband jokes that they are a captive audience who can't go anywhere so they have to deal with me. It proves that you can build friendships through honest conversation, even if you have to do it with Plexi-glass and bars between you and the other person.'

Gale is a British lady in her early sixties who moved to Thailand with her husband and children in 1997 when his company posted him in Bangkok. Initially, she became involved in helping out at a rural school, which her husband's company sponsored. Although the Thai school was in the middle of nowhere, it was relatively clean and well equipped with basic facilities and equipment. The pupils, however, came from impoverished households and had neither proper shoes nor uniforms, she says. Gale was touched by the children's enthusiasm.

She said: 'I had tears in my eyes, seeing how happy the kids were to see us and how appreciative they seemed to be to receive small gifts we had prepared for them. Each of them received a goody bag of crisps, a book and a pencil. Afterwards, they were in for a treat of ice-cream as well. Back in the UK, had I given a child the same gift bag they would probably have said, "Is that all?" It was very humbling to see these children appreciate the little kindness so much. I've been to many schools since then to make donations, do activities with the students or host parties for them.'

Through a network of friends at the British Women's Group in Bangkok and the British Community in Thailand Foundation for the Needy, Gale started to participate in other volunteer work, including spring cleaning at the Aids hospice in the slum of Klong Toey. Later another British woman who had been visiting prisoners on death row at the Bangkok Hilton asked Gale and her friend Katherine Biggs to accompany her to the prison. She was about to leave Thailand and wanted someone to carry on this duty. Gale agreed immediately. Her first visit proved an eye-opener.

She said: 'We visited three inmates, two of whom were on death row. The men came to see us with shackles on their ankles. It was very daunting to see them in that state as I had never seen anybody being treated like that before. We didn't ask too much but obviously were interested in how they had ended up in a place like this. They were all in there for drug offences.

'We left the prison feeling quite emotional. Katherine turned to me and said, "We'll have to come here again, won't we?" I said yes and I've come here for four years now. My attitude is that, no matter what they are now, they are somebody's son or brother or uncle. I can sympathise as a mother because—God forbid—if it were my son being incarcerated 6,000 miles away from home, it would mean a lot to me if there were someone on the other end to check up on his wellbeing and send me an email, telling me he is all right and that he sends his love.'

During her first visits, Gale noticed the so-called 'banana visitors' who go into the prison simply to satisfy their curiosity.

'Sadly, some young tourists just want to come to Bang Kwang and gawk. They come here so they can brag about the experience later to their friends back home. Some even made promises to keep in touch with the inmates they visited but they didn't. On the other hand, some who came as tourists ended up building long-term friendships with the inmates.

'In general, I think these visits benefit both the tourists and the inmates. The inmates remind them of their freedom and choices they could make in their lives. Obviously, the tourists can learn from their mistakes and be warned of what could happen during their stay.'

When people approach Gale and asked her what it is like to visit the Bangkok Hilton, she invites them to see for themselves. It is not everyone's cup of tea, however, and for some one visit is enough.

'Mostly I pass messages between the chaps and their families. Sometimes the families give me money to get things that their sons need. Being a messenger doesn't sound much but I live here so I can speed up the communication between them. I can send an email from a chap to his family and get a reply for him within a week. If they use letters, it could be at least three weeks in turnaround time. The families said it makes all the difference for them knowing that there is somebody who is on the outside to check that their sons or brothers are all right.

'When I'm back in England, I visit some of the families if they don't live too far from where I am. Other families call me while I'm there as well. They don't phone me while I'm here because of the difference in time. We communicate mainly via email since it costs next to nothing. When the families visit Bangkok we always meet up and I take photographs of the families and send them to the chaps as well.'

Gale's help isn't limited to British inmates.

'I met some Hong Kong Chinese and British nationals [overseas]. One of the British guys was friendly with a Burmese inmate. It was after Nagris [a cyclone that caused hundreds of thousands of fatalities in Burma in 2008] when he asked me to ring this Burmese chap's brother to find out if his family was safe and I have been in contact with his brother since.

'We chipped in to buy a wheelchair for a Hong Kong man who had no support after having a stroke. I used to send in some toiletries to the chaps, knowing they would distribute them to Thai or Cambodian inmates who don't have any support. It is just a little gesture when we think about it in normal circumstances but a small bottle of shampoo or shower gel could make an inmate feel really clean for the first time in a long while. Our guys help those who are less fortunate than they are as well.'

In one case, a Malaysian inmate who had become a valued staff member at the hospital, got a Burmese prisoner transferred from his building to the prison hospital, with help from the prison's chief doctor. The Burmese man had shown signs of mental illness following rapes and assaults by other inmates. Staying at the hospital meant he was out of his abusers' reach and could receive some basic treatment. Later a church group in the prison hospital, headed by a Thai inmate, took him under its wing.

Some inmates try to help the less fortunate ones. I guess these are the few who do get some rehabilitation. Some Asian inmates form friendships with the *farang* (foreign) ones. They know they have a better chance of surviving in Bang Kwang if they stick to their white friends as they have contact with outsiders. So they wash their clothes and do errands for them.

I asked Gale if any inmate she visited had ever confided in her about their experiences inside the Bangkok Hilton. To my surprise, she said so far none of them had told her any horrific stories and it was unlikely that they were subjected to any abuse since they are westerners and are treated better than other nationalities such as Thai, Cambodian or Burmese.

She said: 'From what I've heard from the chaps, it's more frustration than anything else that they have to deal with. Thing such as requests for medical treatment don't happen quickly or even at all—even after they go through the red tape. Communication with the Thai authorities sometimes gets lost in translation. Sometimes they just give up because it is too much of hassle to get even one request.'

Gale offered a rather amusing story instead.

'A chap told me that he had been watching *Psycho* one night and he couldn't sleep afterwards. I said, "Are you kidding? It was only a film but you live among murderers, rapists and the likes." I found it funny for him to be so scared of a film but he didn't seem to realise what a grim reality he was in. But I suppose the inmates, be they westerners or Asians, form some kind of comradeship and they forget the reason why the others are in there. He and I had a big laugh before he said, "For God's sake, Gale, if I thought like that, I would never sleep a wink." It is scary to think that you have to sleep next to a person who has knifed or shot someone, isn't it?'

Given the harsh conditions inside Thai prisons, I assumed the foreign inmates would prefer to be sent back to their own countries where prison life would be more tolerable if possible. A British inmate has to serve four years in a Thai jail before he becomes eligible for transfer under the bilateral prisoner transfer agreement. The process can take about a year to complete. Transferred inmates have to serve half of the remaining Thai sentence in a British prison before they become eligible for a parole under UK law. The surprise is that some British inmates don't want to be transferred back home, says Gale.

'Some chaps told me that the prisoner transfer treaty between Thailand and UK is a problem for them. I was told that prisoners from other western countries are freed much sooner than the British are after their transfers. Say a British person is given 30 years by a Thai court, he will have to serve at least four years here before he can serve half of the remaining time in a UK prison. There he will be subject to British law, which means he will be entitled to parole after serving half of his sentence or six years and six months. Altogether, he will serve at least 10 years and six months, even though he wouldn't get such a harsh sentence for killing his own child in the UK.'

Gale's comparison between sentences given for drug smuggling in Thailand and sentences given to the 'baby killers' struck a chord with me and, on further research, I read several disturbing cases of fathers killing their infants. One account etched in my mind is of Mark Howe, who was found guilty of punching or kicking his 18-month-old daughter's stomach with such force that tore her intestines. He left her to die slowly the following day when, had he taken her to the hospital, she might have been saved. An English judge sentenced him to only five years in prison.

I am puzzled by the lenience shown these 'baby killers' while Gale is puzzled by the harsh sentences handed down to drug offenders in Thailand. However, Gale and I agree that it really comes down to the law of the land.

She said: 'Had the chaps committed similar offences in the UK, they could have served just a small portion of the Thai sentence. I think the time the British offenders serve in Thailand is enough for the crime they commit. One of the guys I visited was sentenced to 26 years, when he would have probably have served only six months if judged in a British court. Plus, they suffer the extra trauma of being so far away from their families.

'Moreover, when they go back, because they were handed high sentences by Thai courts, they are categorised as high-risk inmates and put in high-security prisons. Some of the older prisons in the UK I visited are in a pretty awful state. There is a serious shortage of guards so the inmates can be locked up in their cells for most of the day in the UK. In Bang Kwang, they are allowed some freedom to walk about, exercise, write letters and read for about eight hours a day.'

Western inmates usually are left to their own devices and they don't have to work in factories, as do the Thai inmates, so they have more free time. The non-Asian inmates tend to write letters of complaint as well.

Not being able to choose which part of Britain they will end up in has made some reluctant to ask for a transfer, she says.

'They can apply for a specific prison but there is no guarantee they will get the one they want. Obviously they prefer the prisons where their families and friends could visit them often. Given where the treaty stands now, some of them prefer to stay here despite the harsh living conditions.

'Here they are more or less left on their own. They are unlikely to be the subject of assault or to be victimised by the guards or the other inmates. I think they are in a better position here compared to at home where they would be treated as ordinary inmates. The weather is also a big factor. The weather in the UK is freezing cold compared to the warm weather in Thailand.

'Of course, not all the British inmates feel this way about the treaty. I went to see one chap who had been transferred back to a fairly new prison. The place was modern, clean and private-run. Some of the guys had done a spell in UK prisons before and they knew what it was like to be locked up in a high security prison. Being transferred back to the UK is not the best option for some of them though.'

Most prisoners accept the punishment they are handed out, she says. 'I'm sure they knew the law but they took a terrible risk, thinking they could get away with it. While I think the penalty for drug offenders here is too high, I understand it is the law of the land and I respect that. Foreigners are guests here, therefore we should follow the law of the land.

'If you choose to live in a foreign country, you should be respectful to the hosts and their culture. It bothers me whenever another foreigner complains and moans about Thailand. If they don't like Thailand, then they should go and live somewhere else. If you want to live here, you have to embrace Thailand entirely. I love how Thai people generally treat me with respect.'

Another veteran foreign inmate visitor told me there are other reasons why some convicts don't want to be transferred back to their countries. Some had been long-term expatriates in Thailand living with Thai wives and children before they were incarcerated, so being sent back would mean uprooting the lives they have created here.

Some Africans don't want to be sent back to their own countries simply because the prison conditions there are even worse. I have heard that some inmates regard Bang Kwang literally as the Bangkok Hilton.

The other factor, which is often overlooked, is race. In general, Caucasian foreigners are treated better in Thailand and they are given certain protection because the guards just let them be. If they go back to their own countries, they would be treated as ordinary inmates.

From talking to several *farang* volunteers, what seems to be a source of frustration for them is that the regulations on visiting are changed from time to time. Each director is different in terms of opening the prison to the outsiders. I've worked with one who invited comedians inside to entertain the inmates and another who didn't even want anyone to take photos or videos of the prison from the outside.

Although they may differ in approach, all they want is that the prison runs smoothly during their tenure. The authorities make more rules as they go along because the inmates find new and clever ways to break the rules. At the time of interview, Gale told me no parcels were allowed to be sent inside because a mobile phone SIM card had been found hidden inside a pizza. This meant she could not take in '*farang* food' such as tins of tuna or corned beef.

Sometimes Gale is told to change seats by prison guards a few times without giving her a reason before she can sit and talk. When she finally sits down, she finds that the phone doesn't work and has to find another seat. Despite these little sources of frustration, she says the prison staff treat her group well in general and the inmates haven't complained too much.

'Thailand allows me to be more charitable. I can just go out and help people. You cannot do this in some developed countries due to red tape. Overall, it has been a humbling experience for me. I don't volunteer to have people say I'm wonderful. I do it because I enjoy it and want to do it. And I also believe what goes round comes round. My father, who was a prisoner of war and an undertaker, told me the greatest gift you can give to someone is your time and I guess I heed his words.

'When I get email from one of the chaps' families in the morning, I'll print it out to tell the chap he's got a message from his family, reminding him that he has not been forgotten. It feels great being the bearer of good news and being in a position to help others. I think you can get much, if not more, from giving than receiving, seeing happy faces of those you've helped. I'm sure a lot of people would feel the same.'

Given that the authorities discover drugs hidden in incoming parcels for the inmates from time to time, the guards can't be too sure about the motives of all the visitors. Officials at the Bangkok Hilton are on the lookout for any visitors who may be involved in the drug trade or illicit dealings—be they individuals or faith-based groups. Crackdowns on drug rings on the outside are sometimes linked to the drug trade inside the prisons.

Cynicism is prevalent. One charity group, which is staffed by Thais and Asians, is said to be running a money-making scheme. First, they tend to spend more time with rich inmates. Allegedly, the staff compile lists of items that the prisoners want and go about finding companies that can donate these items. They then fabricate receipts to show that they bought these items with donors' money. So much for charity.

My last title at Bang Kwang was Chief of the Foreign Affairs division and it was a great opportunity for me to meet many westerners who had committed to helping inmates of their own nationality and others. Dealing with hardened criminals and piles of documents could be tedious, so meeting them was a pleasure.

I'm glad to call some of them my friends and have welcomed them into my life. They have worked with the Thai officials to organise many projects to improve the living conditions of the inmates. These individuals are the side of the Bangkok Hilton that should be told of more.

Chapter 5

LIFE INSIDE THE BANGKOK HILTON

Bang Kwang is a society like no other, with its own set of rules. Its residents, the inmates, vary in terms of fortune, background and nationality, with 40 countries represented.

There are small-time drug smugglers from tribal villages in the north of Thailand, Chinese drug barons, former army generals, high-ranking ex-police officers, a once-revered monk and at least three doctors.

Within this confined world, there is a class system, just like in the outside world. If you happen to be at the lower end of the scale, you may end up to doing demeaning things to survive because there is little support available.

The long sentences mean that, at best, prisoners spend many years behind bars. At worst, they never get out. So over time the support of their loved ones often fades away and they are forgotten or abandoned. Often Thai wives ask for a divorce or simply take new husbands so that they have someone to provide for themselves and their children. Some inmates vent their anger and resentment through self-harm: cutting their fingers, starving themselves or taking drugs. A few go as far as committing suicide.

Outsiders say life in Bang Kwang is cruel and there is a lot of temptation to engage in illicit activities, so you cannot expect the inmates to change. The odds are stacked against them.

However, I think these circumstances can be a true test of character. For those inmates who face down temptation and get by through honest means, it can be a way to reform. They have my respect.

As I have always said, not all the inmates are evil. People commit crimes for a number of reasons: rage, desperation, foolishness or greed.

Whatever landed them in the Bangkok Hilton says less about their character than how they choose to live when inside. There are many inmates who get by as honestly and productively as they can. The prison provides just the bare necessities of life, so the inmates have to use what skills they have to make a living.

Those who have legal expertise are in high demand as the hope of getting out occupies the minds of the detainees all the time. So a number have pursued law degrees while incarcerated. They give legal advice and write letters of complaint and petitions for individual royal pardon for the others. Most of those on death row hire their fellow inmates to write petitions for them instead of their lawyers, who they usually grow to mistrust.

Former Muay Thai (kick-boxing) practitioners teach others about the lethal martial art and also work as masseurs. The boxers have learnt how to massage so that they can relax the muscles and relieve pain. A good masseur can earn a decent income inside because there are plenty of clients, including prison guards. One who did this was Payak. Famed for his strong punch, he claims he hadn't intended to kill anybody, though he was convicted of murder. Payak says he was enslaved by his addiction to a life of indulgence, which took every last satang in his pocket. When he needed money, he would rob somebody. His luck ran out when he tried to steal an expensive-looking necklace from a woman and she died during the struggle. He is now a sought-after masseur.

Fortune-tellers do well too because prisons are full of people who feel unlucky and are bothered by questions about their lives. They are paid in cigarettes, snacks or food. There same questions come up time and again. When will I be released? Will the next court dismiss my case? Will I receive good news about my individual petition for royal pardon? When will the next mass royal pardon come and how much of a reduction will I get in my sentence?

Prison guards also consult them about the possibility of promotion, family and love. Usually, after a reading the fortune-teller suggests the client make merit or go to see a monk for a blessing in order to improve their luck.

A lot of inmates are killers from impoverished backgrounds. They don't have the support of their families who are scraping by just as they are. Some of them become cooks to make a living. It is a strange sight to see murderers covered in tattoos attentively selecting ingredients and cooking fried fish, curries and desserts. They order the ingredients from prison shops or from prisoners who work on farms.

One former hitman, who has killed a number of people, turned his hand to cultivating vegetables as he has no family that can help him out. He was on the run with his heavily pregnant wife when the police caught him. A few months into his incarceration, his wife left his child with his mother and never returned. His mother barely has enough money to support a young child, let alone her adult son. He says all the money he used to make from killing was cursed as if an unseen force compelled him to use up the blood money wastefully. Once the last satang was out of his pocket, he just took another job. So he had no resources to dip into while in prison.

Just when he was at his most desperate, as luck would have it, he noticed an empty plot of land in the compound near his building and this gave him an idea. He asked a guard for permission to create a vegetable patch. When somebody who used to kill people in cold blood for hefty fees starts cultivating food instead, that shows he is turning over a new leaf.

Generally, those who don't have skills approach influential and wealthy inmates known as the *khayai* (big legs) and offer to be their servants. These big legs come from rich families or used to be high-ranking policemen or soldiers. They provide for less fortunate inmates in return for their services as cleaners.

The 'servants' wash clothes, dishes and tidy the master's *baan* (house), which is really just the small space away from the cells the inmate has claimed ownership over and uses as a spot to relax during the daytime. A house can be a gathering place for inmates of the same group or nationality or even a 'couple'.

Opportunistic guards try to get into the big legs' good books as well. They befriend them for such reasons as career advancement or special favours. Big legs who used to be politicians, policemen, soldiers or state officials don't lose their connections with bigwigs on the outside. They boast to the guards about their ability to pull strings to secure promotion or re-assignment for them to other places.

To validate their association, some guards claim to be related to big legs by blood or to have something in common with them such as coming from the same hometown or sharing the same ancestors hundreds of years ago. Some inmates are so wealthy and powerful, the guards end up offending each other while vying to impress them.

In Bang Kwang, not only is the character of each prisoner put to the test, but so is the character of each guard. More often than not, new guards are targets of inmates who try to befriend them, albeit with ulterior motives.

A guard's first days in Bang Kwang can be intimidating and so the friendliness offered by the inmates can be welcome initially.

First, the prisoners try to find out where the newcomers are from so they can establish links with those from the same region. Each part of Thailand has its own dialect and it is easier for them to communicate in it.

To make the new guards warm towards them, the inmates offer to make coffee, prepare snacks and give them cigarettes. Slowly, any doubts the guards may have over the sincerity of the prisoners erodes. Once the inmates are sure the bond is strong enough, they start asking the guards to return their favours with small requests such buying items for them, contacting their relatives on their behalf or secretly sending letters for them to avoid the screening. The guards who are too naïve find themselves in a dilemma because if they fulfil these seemingly innocent requests, they will violate prison rules. If they refuse, however, they will be accused of being ungrateful. Kickbacks are offered in return for carrying out risky requests such as trafficking in alcohol, cash, mobile phones, narcotics or other prohibited items.

When I was in charge of the trustees, I arrested several inmates who were dealing drugs. One investigation led to two prison guards who had brought in the drugs. They said they needed a lot of money to get married. Given their low salaries, I could sympathise with them—but it doesn't excuse their crimes.

Using information from trustees, I caught a number of drug-dealers inside Bang Kwang, until a senior prison guard told me off for arresting one of his *dek* (subordinates). He was offended that I had caused trouble for his guy. For all I know, the trustees may have been using me to destroy the networks of their rivals so that one drug ring could monopolise the trade inside. I realised then I could have put myself in danger so I was glad when I was reassigned to another division.

Inmates who befriend guards can also receive protection from bullies. Some prisoners boast about their wealth or the connections they have with important people on the outside to get the guards interested in them. To be on the safe side, some guards befriend them in case they might need a special favour in the future.

Those who have the resources often get their relatives to pay 'protection money' to the guards to ensure their safety. Others ask for a private meeting with a high-ranking officer to show that they have powerful connections. This ploy does not always work.

At one such a meeting, the inmate showed a business card to the warden. On it was the name of a bigwig, his rank and title. Obviously, the inmate wanted to convince the warden that he knew important people. The warden was not impressed by the card and said, 'Since his big friend wants to entrust us with him we should make sure he is going nowhere. Shackle him.'

The inmate's face dropped while the guards tried to muffle their laughter.

On the other hand, however, some flex their muscle successfully. One such inmate had his family get a high-ranking officer to visit him at the prison. Upon hearing of this, the warden arranged for him to meet the inmate in an air-conditioned office instead of the open-air visiting area and the warden himself joined them. Their conversation took place behind closed doors but what is certain is that the inmate's status soared to new heights afterwards.

Those without resources or connections offer to work for the guards for free giving massages, washing clothes, shining shoes or buckles. Like I've said, the guards are *nai* (masters). It is a relationship based on indebtedness and gratitude. On the one hand, it can lead to illicit activities but, on the other hand, some guards have established respectful and amicable relationships with the inmates as well. I find it odd, though, when I see young guards joining the inmates in playing music or games of football or table tennis.

The Corrections Department does not approve of prisoners and guards getting too close. It could discourage this easily by offering better wages and conditions. Entry-level guards are paid badly and yet have to live with the daily temptation to make money through illicit deals. In times of need, people are more inclined to do take risks.

This is a sensitive issue because not all such relationships are interest-based and they don't necessarily lead to illicit deals.

I remember one well-respected old guard who was very hands-on when it came to the welfare of the prisoners. He made sure they received equal portions of food and told the cooks not to favour their friends by giving them the choice pieces of meat while serving watery soup to the others.

When there were riots, the guards who had earned the respect of the inmates through their conduct were asked politely to leave the building. The rest of the time, they were given massages by young prisoners.

One senior guard in his fifties receives a massage on a regular basis. He changes his guard uniform for a *sarong* and sits in a foldup beach chair while his masseur, who is convicted of murder, manipulates muscles in his back and neck.

You probably wouldn't let a killer get his hands around your neck. In Thai culture, however, it is considered very kind for a child to treat parents or grandparents who complain of bad joints to a massage. So this means the prisoner has come to see the guard as an older relative.

I think forming bonds with inmates is risky. There have been some incidents where the guards were penalised for fulfilling benign requests.

One incident involved a guard who was punished for phoning a family on behalf of an inmate to remind them that the deadline for submitting a request for an individual royal pardon was drawing near and if they missed it he would surely be executed.

Aside from opportunities to make a living, the prisoners can also get some education. Bang Kwang is like a multi-disciplinary school. There are official correspondence courses available through the

Basic Education Commission Office and Sukhothai Thammathirat Open University. Prisoners can also learn practical skills at the prison factories or from other inmates that they may be able to use to rebuild their lives after prison.

One former doctor who murdered his wife taught other inmates to help out medical staff at the prison hospital. His license to practise medicine had been revoked and it was against the rules to allow him to do so, but the reality is that, despite his conviction, his knowledge remains. It would be a waste not to allow him to put it to good use.

Not all of them choose to be constructive. Some learn such skills as how to get rid of a body, to remove gun powder, to dismember a body, to pick a lock pick or to steal a car.

No wonder some inmates leave Bang Kwang worse than they were when they arrived. Most of the convicts are between 25 to 35 years old when they arrive and have to serve at least 30 years old in jail. So they have ample time to pick up new interests.

Being a servant may seem demeaning to some but some stoop even lower to survive by becoming *nong* (a term of endearment for female) of inmates who have the resources. *Nongs* are provided for by their 'husbands' in exchange for providing sexual relief. Of course, there are what Thai people call *kathoeys* (effeminate homosexuals or transsexuals) who assume the role of wife.

The difference between these two groups is that *nongs* identify themselves as heterosexual men. Most of *nongs* choose to go against their nature out of necessity as their families are unable to support them or have rejected them. A few choose to become *nongs* to fund their drug addiction, while some go down this path because it seems the easiest way for them to survive. They are in short supply so if not provided for well, *nongs* and *kathoeys* move on to more generous patrons. It is a seller's market and buyers who make the best offer win.

Man-on-man action reportedly takes place during the lockdown after midnight when most inmates are asleep and the temperature has cooled down. The couple claims a spot in the corner of their cell. They set up a love nest with pieces of cloth to shield them from the prying eyes of their cellmates. Those who can afford a partner and a spot for a love nest are rich. Less discreet couples do it underneath a big blanket, poke their heads out when they finish and pretend nothing had happened.

Several *nongs* who were heterosexual men with wives and kids when they first arrived became feminised versions of themselves after assuming the role of *nong* for too long. Some even become full-fledged *kathoeys*. The family of one *nong*, name Sithi, received quite a shock when they visited him after several years without contact.

Out of the blue, he was informed that his parents, wife and child had come to see him. For any other inmate, this news would have been welcomed with nothing but joy. It was as much a cause of concern as of happiness for Sithi, however, when he met them.

He paid his respects to his parents at their feet and hugged his wife and child. They were in shock and remained silent, however, because the smooth-skinned man with hairless arms and legs they saw was a stranger to them. Sithi sheepishly assured his parents that he was their son.

Although they can be strained, contact visits are important in giving the inmates hope that they can be reunited with their families one day. Such visits take place twice a year and are special occasions for the prisoners. It gives them something to live for.

During one such occasion, a wheelchair-bound elderly Chinese man was waiting for his relatives who used to fly to Thailand to visit him every year without fail. This time, however, there was no sign of them. He suffered a heart attack and was rushed to the prison hospital. He passed away there. Perhaps, what he saw around him—people hugging, crying tears of joy and eating together—and the thought that he had been forgotten brought on the attack. His relatives arrived minutes later and, instead of a happy reunion, they tearfully collected his body.

It can be lonely inside even though it is overcrowded. There are about 20 inmates sharing one cell and sometimes more. The lack of privacy is one way to prevent bad incidents from happening, however. If there is a fight, there will be witnesses. If a detainee seems suicidal, others will try to talk him out of it. Those thinking of escaping will find plenty of inmates who try to stop them as they know that if there is a break-out, their lives will become harder because the rules will be enforced more strictly. Lights are on all night during the lockdown and this troubles many inmates, especially the foreigners who complain that they cannot sleep and that the lights damage their eyes.

At the other extreme are the hardened criminals. These men continue to make a living inside from committing acts of violence or even murder. They call themselves samurai and rich inmates hire them to kill or assault their opponents. Moneylenders hire them to teach their debtors a lesson if they miss a repayment.

They have nothing left to lose and their chances of getting out are slim. They are either serving life sentences or have cases awaiting should they get out. They are not afraid of getting a longer sentence or being downgraded as they are already classified as the lowest in the prison. They don't mind failing to get a sentence reduction when a mass royal pardon takes place. They don't care about having their rights to see visitors taken away as their families have already disowned them.

However they choose to spend their time, there is a lot of it. So the inmates find activities to distract themselves from the tedium of captivity. Some of them exercise, play musical instruments, watch TV or pet the many cats that live there too. The cats were brought in originally to combat a rat problem. Over time, their numbers have multiplied. These days, the animals serve as companions to the inmates more than predators of vermin. A fight can break out if an inmate harms a cat that is dear to another.

Some inmates train the cats to carry small items, such as packets of instant coffee or cigarettes, to their friends in the next cell. They attach the items with adhesive tape onto the cat's neck. Some years ago, an inmate was caught using his cat as a drug-runner. He taped the delivery onto its belly and somehow the feline managed to take the drug to his client in another building.

Some of them use the downtime to assert their sense of self and gain recognition from their peers though, for example, getting tattoos. In Thai culture, tattoos have magic powers. Having a tattoo is like carrying a talisman on your body. In ancient times, soldiers believed tattoos could protect them against sharp weapons, making their skin impenetrable and them indestructible. Fast-forward to the present day Bangkok Hilton and it serves a new purpose. Some young, good-looking newcomers told me they didn't care about aesthetics or occult powers as long as the ink on their bodies made them less desirable targets for rape by the senior inmates. Tattoos can also represent gang insignia.

Some inmates also pass the time by engaging in a very disturbing activity: genital mutilation. I've been told that there are three types of penis mutilation in Bang Kwang. The first is called 'Benz-surgery', whereby the head is scarred so that it will look like the Mercedes-Benz logo when it heals. Inmates who get their genitals scarred in this way claim they are men's men. Well, the prison version. How they come to that conclusion is beyond me.

The second type is called 'bury pearls'. The skin is cut, small balls are inserted and it is sewn up again. In the past, the inmates used to break plastic bottle caps into pieces and then rub those bits against the cement floor until they became tiny balls. Now they use ready-made plastic balls. Some inmates are sick enough to 'bury pearls' several times. This takes a long time since they have to allow the skin to heal between one insertion and the next. Some make two cuts to put in two balls at once to save time.

The third kind is called 'install bud'. The name doesn't really reflect how it is done. Basically, they make several small cuts on the penis, which turn into scars. This makes the skin uneven and scary-looking.

Of course, those who make mistakes are permanently disfigured—though not in the way they wanted to be. These 'operations' are carried out in secrecy and the equipment is not sanitary. Often they have inflammation and swelling. They cannot wear pants so they wear sarongs while their cuts are healing. The more serious cases are sent to the prison hospital.

It is beyond me why these inmates choose to mutilate themselves when the prison provides more productive options for them. Those who do these things don't seem to think that they are harming themselves but see this hideous practice as a way to assert themselves among their peers and to show their bravado.

Bang Kwang holds the country's most hardened criminals and tension between them is high as they all try to prove they are the strongest. Clashes are commonplace and often bloody fights erupt, sometimes resulting in death. The attackers are penalised according to the severity of their actions. They may be shackled, put in solitary confinement or refused visitors for one to three months. Those who kill someone inside are prosecuted by the courts and get an additional sentence. Some lifers or death row inmates couldn't care less if they get another year in jail.

In general, what the inmates fear most is being downgraded to a lower category. The inmates are classified into six categories according to how well they behave: excellent, very good, good, normal, bad and very bad. Some deserve to be put into a seventh category as they have killed a lot of people. Bang Kwang holds the upgrading test twice every year.

When a mass royal pardon is handed out, those in the first class will have their sentences cut by half. Those in the second class will get a two-thirds reduction. The third class gets a one-third cut. The fourth class get a quarter off and the bad inmates a fifth. The very bad ones get none.

In the past, the convicts viewed killers and rapists as the lowest kind and their penalty was to be raped, bullied and looked down upon by their fellow inmates because they were not real men and had committed atrocities against *pedmae* (mother's gender).

Some prisoners got back at their opponents by finding ways to attack them without their knowing. A prison guard told me once that an injured inmate came to him for help with a soft tin box covering his head. As he got closer to him, his nose detected a revolting smell and he could see human excrement dripping from the box. The guard quickly ordered the trustees to remove the box from the man's head but they were understandably reluctant to do so. The choice of human waste box was obviously to inflict maximum humiliation on his victim.

The trustees cleaned him up as much as they could. The box was little bigger than the man's head and there were jagged edges designed to scratch his face as it was being removed. So they carefully and slowly took it off.

This smelly, vicious attack was a new twist on an old trick. Underhand attackers usually put sacks of thick cloth over the heads of their targets before beating them up instead of having face-to-face fistfights. Obviously, they get away with this because their victims cannot identify who attacked them.

Not all prisoners are so clever. The afternoon before I was put in charge of the trustees, or the 'blue shirts' as they are called by the ordinary inmates in brown, a friendly senior guard named Paisarn called me into his office for a briefing. He told me of a stabbing incident in which a man ran back to his cell after badly wounding a bully. The poor guy held out the homemade knife he had made from a metal rod threateningly while yelling: 'I'll fight whoever the heck walks in. I'll fight!'

Until this day, I don't understand why he ran back into his cell. Paisarn was unmoved and coldly called out: 'Drop your weapon and I promise no one will hurt you. Otherwise I will be forced to teach you a lesson.'

Standing behind him were blue-shirted inmates who were eager to deliver a hiding on his behalf. Although he was scared, the poor guy kept repeating his pitiful threat. With a nod from Paisarn, the trustees produced thick bamboo sticks and inserted them through the spaces between the bars. They manipulated the sticks deftly to hit him repeatedly. He was smacked around from one side of the cell to the other like a piece of sweat-soaked rag until he gave up with a whimper.

Paisarn stopped short of revealing what happened next to the man, rolled a cigarette and puffed on it. Then he said: 'The man may have been wronged by the guy he stabbed for all I care but we have rules here and we need to enforce them. He didn't drop the weapon so I had to make him.'

He then told me of a similar incident where the attacker had climbed onto the roof of an outdoor toilet and vowed to fight to the death only to have stones hurled at him by the trustees.

He continued: 'You see my point is, some people just need to be hurt first before they can listen to you… and another thing you need to know is to let them be—but not too comfortably. They can complain about how hard their life inside is. Just remind them that this place is designed to punish them and they have no right to demand things because they are the bad guys.'

So I asked him: 'What should I do if things get out of hand—like if there is a big gang fight or a riot?'

He replied: 'You wouldn't rub gold onto rough stone, would you? It's beneath you to get involved. The best policy is to wait until it has cleared. Let the trustees handle the troublemakers. They're a tough bunch and that's what they are for. If anyone is hurt or worse, you can always say it was done in the melee by trustees acting outside your orders. This is no game and you can't be a hero. One guard tried to stop a fight. He got stabbed in the hand and lost the use of it forever. Think about what your wife and children would do if anything should happen to you.'

I soon came to realise what it felt like to have an army of my own but I was conscious about how I wielded a force that is a double-edged sword. Back then, the trustees were selected from 'excellent' class inmates who had a background in military or police service. They had to be well-behaved to be assigned the title.

Prisoners outnumbered guards dramatically, so the trustees were valuable in keeping control as well as infiltrating criminal activities. I found most of them to be decent people. While they were rewarded with their own less-crowded lodgings and better sentence reductions whenever a mass amnesty took place, they were also the target of attacks by drug-dealers and others who saw them as betraying their own kind.

After arresting drug-dealers inside, I would be summoned to Nonthaburi court, as the prison is within its jurisdiction. The most common question from the judge was: 'How does a forbidden substance get smuggled into the prison in the first place? Given the protocol of screening everything, is it possible the prison guards helped to bring it in?'

I would reply: 'Your honour, the prisoners still have contact with outsiders and guards. Of these people, surely some do facilitate drug-smuggling.'

After two young prison guards were arrested for smuggling drugs into the prison, I caught a number of drug-dealers inside using the intelligence they gave me.

The status of trustees is different now. Their role has been reduced but still inmates vie for the title because of the extra sentence reduction. Some affluent Thai inmates pull strings to become trustees, so they are not necessarily a brutal force any more.

Certain groups of inmates, who are considered to be a different class, are the *farang* (foreigners). In general, they are left to their own devices and have a place to gather during the day. They read books, write letters and relax. The *farangs* are considered big complainers in the eyes of the prison guards and they are always finding fault with the living conditions. The African inmates tend to make claims about human rights violations, especially over the use of shackles, as they represent slavery. When dealing with complaints from foreign inmates, obviously the authorities take into account bilateral relations in making any compromises.

In general, foreign Asian inmates are obedient and don't complain much. The majority of inmates from Burma, Laos and Cambodia are small-time drug-smugglers who come from poor backgrounds. Inmates of Chinese descent are perceived to be rich from running international drug rings. So they are welcomed by opportunistic guards and inmates alike. They can keep their wealth intact, unlike the Thais whose assets are confiscated unless they have been clever enough to get somebody to buy gold or diamonds.

Slowly they ask someone on the outside to sell these assets to fund their lives inside. They often receive help and support from their families in the form of money, parcels and visits. Their relatives also send in such traditional Chinese delicacies as shark's fin, shiitake mushrooms, sea cucumber, fish maw and herbs. Sometimes food parcels arrive with roasted pork, grilled chicken or duck in vacuum bags. The Chinese inmates prepare dishes for the guards to win their approval. Given that they come from similar cultural backgrounds and because of their generosity, they get along well with Thai inmates and guards while westerners and Africans tend to stay within their own groups.

Spending too many years behind bars can cost inmates their sanity. Several have become mentally instable. One man attacked a guard with a broom until his head bled. Afterwards, he explained: 'Last night I dreamt he hit me. So when I woke up this morning I decided to take revenge.'

Speaking of revenge, there are ways the inmates can get back at hated guards without them knowing. To them, the guards can be their saviour or a nightmare. Obviously, the guards who really listen to their problems and settle disputes between prisoners fairly are preferred and are rewarded by having their clothes washed for free or a massage.

The inmates conceal their resentment for those who make life harder for them. They will still be served coffee but it will have spit in it. A glass of cold water will get a good stir with a penis. Some guards who know that they are in inmates' bad books take the precautions of ordering only hot water or carrying drinks to work in a thermos.

Thai prisoners are divided into groups according to where they come from: northerners, southerners, north-easterners. Those from the central region don't seem to form an obvious group.

Other groups are based on the type of offence and some types of crime are associated with specific regions. Most drug offenders are northerners or north-easterners as both regions are routes through which narcotics are trafficked into Thailand from neighbouring countries. It is said that hitmen, killers and robbers tend to come from the central region while most of the murderers are from the south.

Religion also brings some together. The three major beliefs in Bang Kwang are Buddhism, Christianity and Islam. Christian and Muslim inmates form obvious groups while the Buddhists don't. Some Muslims once complained when some of their number converted to Christianity to receive donations, an affront to their faith.

When they get together, the inmates gain visibility and some protection against bullies, though clashes between different groups often result in injury.

Most Asian countries don't have prisoner transfer treaties with Thailand. This results in their nationals having to stay behind bars much longer than western or African ones.

Control and limiting the rights of convicts are the main priorities in the Bangkok Hilton—after all it is a place of punishment for convicts. The idea of rehabilitation was introduced much later and seems to be bottom of the priority list. In fact, I sometimes wonder if inmates who have served time in the Bangkok Hilton leave as better people or as hardened criminals. Given the number of notorious gang leaders inside, every day is like a crime seminar in there.

The inmates range from a small-time thieves to crime bosses. All of them have one thing in common: long imprisonment. They have no freedom and are subject to a lot of rules.

We don't allow them to use communication equipment to contact outsiders. Most of them have no mattresses to sleep on, unless they buy their own. They each have to bid for the most lucrative spot in their respective cells—the farthest from the toilet that is. The toilet is just a three-sided knee-high wall that cannot contain the sound of someone breaking wind. They lie side by side.

Those who are awaiting trial on drug charges may have to sleep next to a serial killer. There is simply no privacy. There is access to treatment and medicine but don't bet on getting it quickly. They are searched at least twice a day for 'prohibited items', the obvious ones being opium, cannabis, alcohol, alcohol substitutes, gambling apparatus, escape apparatus (which depends on your interpretation), weapons, perishable or intoxicating items, gasoline and explosives. That list is growing by the minute and the prison has a very straightforward way of adding to it. Say, for example, a guard finds a SIM card cleverly hidden in a pizza, then pizza will be banned. Our concern is that they would conduct drug dealing over mobile phones to get *yaba* into the prisons and sell it to the other prisoners. So the rest of the inmates who innocently crave it can forget about it.

In general, Thailand operates with a kind of caste system. Your surname, wealth, gender, age, skin colour, education and other factors will be taken into consideration by others. It is like we have a mental calculator to help us evaluate each other according to these criteria. Prison operates in pretty much in the same way even though all inmates more or less should be treated equally.

So the inmates have to find ways to better their position inside. The route to power is straightforward for Thais, though foreigners have a more complicated approach.

Generally the big legs use their connections to get their powerful friends to visit them. It is a subtle way to let guards and prisoners alike know they are somebody. After achieving a level of respect from the guards, they start to act as channels of communication between the prisoners and the prison in the regard to donations, complaints and reports from the prisoners. Ordinary inmates pin their hopes on them. When they resolve a problem, they get even more respect from their peers. Though we have taken their freedom they find ways to make life inside more bearable.

Some big legs who were crime bosses on the outside continue to run similar enterprises inside, offering credit, running gambling dens and selling drugs. Poorer inmates often offer to serve them in the hope that they might secure a dubious job or two at one of their businesses after they are released.

That's not to say that Bang Kwang is a safe place. It comes under a lot of scrutiny, however, so violence is less common there than in other less known Thai detention centres such as the one in Pathumthani province.

In 2009, two siblings of a man who died there while being detained for a minor offence took their plight to the media. Their brother had been arrested for drunk driving. He was instructed to pay a fine of 3,000 baht but he had no money on him so he was sentenced to 15 days in a detention centre in Pathumthani province in late of October. On November 1, the centre called to his workplace to say that he was dead and his co-workers called his family.

LIFE INSIDE THE BANGKOK HILTON

The death certificate said he had suffered internal bleeding in his chest, his ribs were broken and both lungs were torn. Given the horrific injuries, his relatives visited officers at the detention centre to ask what had happened. They claimed he fell as he was walking to the bathroom and when they found him on the floor he was already dead.

A similar incident had happened at the same detention centre the previous January. A woman said her husband was beaten to death while in detention.

'My husband was a taxi driver. He was charged with drunk-driving on January 15, 2009. The court gave him seven days in jail and he was sent to the central detention centre for men in Pathumthani. He arrived there on Friday, January 16 to spend his first weekend in jail. On Monday, I was informed by an officer that he had been hospitalised.'

When she asked what happened, the officer replied that he was found unconscious in the morning and sent to a nearby hospital. At the hospital, she found her husband covered in bruises. It appeared to her that he had been beaten about the head. She called to the centre again and this time the officer said her husband had fallen in the bathroom. Her husband was transferred to another hospital for an x-ray. The result confirmed her worst nightmare. They found huge haemorrhaging in his brain but the surgeon said his body was so badly injured he wouldn't survive an operation. The doctor told her to prepare herself for the worst. On January 21, 2009, her husband died and the autopsy report revealed that extensive physical damage had been done to the heart, lungs and kidneys. The damage was far too severe to have been brought on by a simple fall.

I am confident that violence by the guards is a thing of the past at Bang Kwang since all eyes are on it due to its notoriety.

Chapter 6

SCAPEGOATS

M any people have asked me whether I think I have ever executed an innocent person. It is a difficult question and one I feel would be more appropriate to direct to the authorities who went before me in handing down a death penalty. After all, I was just the last link in the chain of the Thai justice system.

I believe the closest I ever came to pulling the trigger on an innocent person happened, thankfully, only once in my life. Four men were on death row for six years for a murder they had not committed. One died while he was detained at Bang Kwang. Another contracted a deadly disease there and died five months after he was released. The third died of cancer a few years after getting out. One sole survivor lives to tell of the shocking travesty of justice that occurred in recent Thai history.

What appeared to be a straightforward homicide turned into one of the most shocking cases of police corruption in Thailand. The vicious murder of the teenage girl paled in comparison to the way the police conducted their investigation and their disregard for four innocent men.

On July 25, 1986, a couple called Sa-ngat and Saiyut Srimuang woke up early and went about their daily work of collecting crabs in a mangrove forest to sell near their home in Samut Prakan province, south of Bangkok. In the forest, they came upon the body of a girl. The Srimuangs called the police immediately who rushed to the scene. The body was identified as that of Sherry Ann Duncan, a Thai-American schoolgirl. She was 16 and had been murdered. The Samut Prakarn police found no wounds on her body and at first they assumed she had died of suffocation, possibly by strangling.

Sherry's parents, Joe and Kloyjai, were questioned first by the police as was Winai Chaipanit, a wealthy businessman in his early forties who was Sherry's lover with the consent of her mother. This kind of relationship is called 'old cow eats young grass' by Thais.

Sherry didn't come from a happy home. Reportedly Joe acted inappropriately towards his daughter, especially when he was drunk. After Winai met Sherry at a restaurant run by Joe and Kloyjai in 1985, Kloyjai decided it was better to allow her daughter to be with Winai as he would support her in every way. So they lived together in a condominium.

Winai reported Sherry's absence to the police on July 26, one day after her body had been found in the mangrove forest. The police also interviewed her classmates who said that after school on the afternoon of July 22, they saw Sherry getting into a taxi that had been waiting for her. They assumed she went home in it as usual. However, none of her classmates remembered the licence plate or saw the driver's face clearly enough to give a description.

The police found themselves in an investigatory cul-de-sac. At the same time, however, the media was covering the story extensively and the angry public demanded that the killers of this young *lukkrueng* (biracial) girl be brought to justice. This resulted in a huge amount of pressure being put on the authorities to solve the case quickly, even though there were no eyewitnesses and the police force did not have the facilities to gather forensic evidence.

After just 27 days, on August 21, 1986, the police arrested five men who were believed to have been involved in the murder, including Winai. Police Lieutenant General Lertlum Thammanisa, the deputy superintendent of Samut Prakan Provincial Police, held a press conference to announce the arrests. The police said Winai had been enraged after he discovered that his teenage lover was seeing another man behind his back, so he paid four of his employees and business associates to kill her. They concluded that Sherry was drugged in the taxi and left to drown at the mangrove forest, which explained why there were no wounds on her body. The five men were arrested at a company that belonged to Winai.

Winai was to be tried as defendant number one. The other four men—Rungchalerm Kanokchawanchai, Pitak Kakhai, Krasae Ployglum and Thawat Kijprayoon—were to stand trial as defendants number two to five.

What led the police to arrest these men was testimony from a key witness named Pramern Potplad, the driver of a three-wheeled *tuk tuk*. He went to see Sherry's mother after he learned about the murder from the papers and later gave his statement to the police on August 20. Pramern said that while driving around the myriad roads of Bangkok looking for business, he came across two men carrying an unconscious girl out of a building, with three men walking behind, in Soi Suan Ploo in Yannawa district of the city. Thinking the girl needed immediate medical attention, Pramern stopped his *tuk tuk* and asked if they wanted a lift to the hospital but the men said no. During the court hearing, Pramern told the judge he vividly remembered the face of the unconscious girl, whom he later knew as Sherry from the papers, because she was a biracial girl with distinctive beauty.

The prosecutor dismissed the charges against Winai due to insufficient evidence on November 6, 1986. However, the Samut Prakan Provincial Court handed down death penalties to the four remaining defendants and they were sent to Bang Kwang. Rungchalerm fainted on hearing the sentence while the other three men and their families were in tears.

Although the murder was high-profile, initially I didn't pay much attention to it as homicide is no stranger to Bang Kwang. Shortly after I started out at the prison in the 1970s, I witnessed the execution of a murderer for the first time in my life. Over the years, you could say I became desensitised to the idea.

That first execution was of a gang-leader named Sa-ne, who was condemned to death by a summary execution order issued by the military government of General Thanom Kittikajorn in 1972. Sa-ne's gang had raped and murdered a 10-year-old girl. They shoved dirt into her mouth to stifle her cries for help and strangled her to death afterwards. The other three members of his gang were let off with life in prison as some of them were as young as 14. Sa-ne wasn't spared as he was above the legal age. He spat vile oaths and curses at the officials who were present at his execution while insisting that he hadn't committed any crime. I was unfortunate enough to witness many more cases like this.

I became interested in the murder of Sherry on hearing that Rungchalerm, one of the four condemned men, had died on October 22, 1991. Shortly afterwards their appeal plea was accepted by the Appeal Court. I hope it offers the tormented soul of Rungchalerm some peace to know that the original verdict was overturned the following January.

Before his passing, I caught only glimpses of his visits with his wife. They both appeared to be inconsolable and in tears most of the time. His health had deteriorated quickly in prison and he was moved to the hospital. A long-term prisoner named Vibul, who was assigned to mind him there, told me that Rungchalerm suffered from asthma, which was exacerbated by trauma and his surroundings. Vibul made light of Rungchalerm's condition, saying it served as a rain forecast because his breathing would be laboured before it rained. Vibul said he regularly injected him with adrenaline to relieve the symptoms.

Vibul was on anti-depression medication and felt particularly drowsy one evening, so he asked another inmate to mind Rungchalerm for him while he went to sleep early. He instructed his replacement that, if Rungchalerm had an asthma attack during the night, he must get him to sit upright on his bed and make him hug a big box and rest on it until the attack went away, as the doctor had recommended.

He was awoken at about 4am by his replacement and rushed to Rungchalerm's bed to find him dead. His replacement claimed that during the night Rungchalerm had an asthma attack and, although he tried to get him to sit up, he resisted his help. Thinking it was not serious, the man just left him. He passed away at the age of 51. The official cause of death was heart failure.

After the Appeal Court overturned the original verdict, the remaining defendants were ordered to be kept on remand while they waited for a ruling by the Supreme Court, except for Krasae, who was granted bail with help from his boss at a security guard company.

In the meantime, Winai, petitioned the National Police Office (now known as the Royal Thai Police) claiming the four men had been convicted wrongfully on false evidence. His petition led to the reinvestigation of this case by a team from the Crime Suppression Division.

On March 8, 1993, the Supreme Court upheld the Appeal Court's verdict and the three men were cleared of murder. They had spent more than six years behind bars.

They were finally set free and I sighed with relief that those innocents would not die at my hands. The suffering of these men and their families was far from over, however.

Pitak contracted tuberculosis during his incarceration and died five months after he was released. The disease had already reached the untreatable stage by then. His mother Intum took her frail son to their hometown of Chiang Mai, a tourist province in northern Thailand, so he could spend the last chapter of his life in peace. They had to live in separate huts so Intum would not catch the disease. Wanting to make his final days happy, she created a garden for her son.

She said, 'My son loved flowers so I bought lots to plant around his hut where he lived next to mine. Visitors all complimented him on how lovely his hut looked.'

Intum, who was in her sixties when she got back a shadow of her son, said, 'He lived with me for five months before I lost him to the disease forever.'

Although it must have been a great comfort for Pitak to know that his mother was always on his side, his paternal relatives held him in contempt for causing the family to lose face, despite his acquittal. They refused to do him the last honour of attending his funeral, so as to express their resentment towards him. Having a quiet funeral is considered a social disgrace in Thailand. Pitak also lost contact with his pregnant wife, whom he never heard from again after he was sent into Bang Kwang.

Thawat had a brief reunion with his family. One of his three daughters, Ratchanee, who was nine when he was arrested, was always adamant that *Por* was innocent in spite of what people around her said.

'My classmates and neighbours said my father was a killer. He suffered so much. Everyone believed the news [that he was guilty], even my grandmother.'

Not only was her father unduly punished, so were she and the rest of the family. Despite Thawat wife's best efforts to support their three daughters, she could not afford to send them to school for long. Two of them finished lower secondary level only while the third just completed primary level. The absence of a 'rice-winner' affected all their futures.

Ratchanee, who finished lower secondary education, said, 'Had my father not been put away, I would have had a chance at higher education.' She earns a living washing clothes while the other two left to find work. As for Thawat, he was unable to find work in Bangkok after he was released and went to work for Winai in the north of Thailand.

In different interviews, Krasae revealed what had happened prior to his wrongful arrest. While being detained, he was subjected to a beating by a group of policemen.

'They asked me to come to the police station and forced me to confess to a crime I didn't commit. I refused and they ganged up on me. There were many of them and I don't recall everything. I remember one police officer in particular who dealt a kick at my chest that was so vicious I fell over, my back hitting a desk behind hard. Then I was kicked in the back again and fell over face down, my head slamming onto the floor.'

Krasae went to see a doctor after the assault and X-rays confirmed that he had cracked his spine. 'I was about to be tried by the court of first instance and I couldn't afford any treatment. [He was a security guard, earning a meagre 3,000 baht a month at the time.] After I was sentenced to death, I was transferred from the court's holding cell to the prison right away.'

While on death row and shackled, he got by with painkillers from the prison hospital and ointment to relax his muscles, sent in by his mother. He also claimed the assault impaired his brain functions and he became slow-witted.

He recalled the time he was on death row saying, 'I didn't know what to think or hope for: to be set free or to die. Drained of any will to live, I was not my own person. I thought, "If it's my time to go, then I'll have no choice but to go." I wasn't even told that another police team was reinvestigating my case to catch the real culprits. There were many kinds of people on death row. Some said they were innocent but got snared by the police who like to close cases quickly. I believe there are innocent people on death row but I don't know how they end up there. The law should guarantee compensation for those who are wrongfully incarcerated.'

Although he is alive and free, Krasae has to live with the constant reminder of the atrocity the police inflicted upon him. 'I still have to take medication to cope with my back pain every day. If I walk for too long, my feet go numb. I can't sleep on my back because doing so is simply too painful and my back goes numb. I have to sleep on either side.' He also admitted to being haunted by an intense fear of the police.

Unlike the other two men, who at the very least had homes to go to after release, Krasae's life after prison was bleak as no one was waiting for his return. He used to live in Klongtoey with his wife, daughter and son. His wife suffered from debilitating depression after he was put behind bars, however, and tried to cope by taking to alcohol, which brought about her untimely death before he was released. His daughter was raped and killed when she was 17 years old, though he was not told of this until after his release. Her killer has not been arrested.

'Had I not been in jail, I would never have let anyone hurt my children,' he cried. His daughter, who was an exceptional student, had been preparing to take an examination for a scholarship to study in Japan before she was murdered. Krasae also lost contact with his son, who went missing.

Krasae became a monk in an attempt to gain solace after the series of tragedies that had befallen him. Some

Thais choose to be ordained as monks or nuns after unfortunate incidents happen in their lives in a bid to start afresh. Krasae eventually returned to secular life, found a partner and work. In order to sustain a hand-to-mouth existence, he took odd jobs that presented themselves including as a Siamese fighting-fish seller and a security guard, which he had been before prison.

About Rungchalerm, Krasae recalled, 'He definitely was the one who took it the hardest among the four of us. He missed his family tremendously—especially his children who were still young at the time he was put away. Not a day went by without him crying... he literally cried himself to death.'

In a poem Rungchalerm wrote in 1991, which unwittingly became the last note to his family, he desperately lamented being jailed for the crime he didn't commit while assuring his children that, even though he had been separated from them, they never left his thoughts.

Tun, his wife, had to take care of their three children, who were between the ages of seven and 11, when her husband was taken away. She found it unbearable trying to console her children, who were being harassed because of their father, and her husband, who couldn't come to grips with his fate. Upon hearing the verdict by the first court, she fainted, as did her husband. Tun visited him twice a week but they are not happy memories, she says.

'It was hell on earth for him. Every visit, we cried and he complained about physical and sexual assaults. The conditions in the prison became unbearable for him and his health deteriorated.'

Supawadee, the eldest child, got a job at a golf course with his undergraduate certificate while the youngest child Rungruengrit had to quit school because Tun couldn't pay for his education. He used his lower secondary certificate to get a job as a messenger. 'If *Por* were with us, our lives would have been better and I could have finished a bachelor degree. He was a hard-working man and we were about to buy a new house and a car,' he said.

Sulaporn, the middle child who was more fortunate than her siblings, got a bachelor degree. She recalled the day the court decided to sentence her father to death.

'The day before, we went out together as a family in high spirits. The next morning *Mae* told us three to go school as usual. She put on a brave face and assured me that *Por* would be home by the evening for sure because he had done nothing wrong. We came home that evening to find out that he would never come home for good. We cried. Five years later, neighbours told us he had died in the prison. It was heartbreaking.'

Rungchalerm's family received some small help from the police. A spokesman for Royal Thai Police asked Sulaporn's university to waive her intuition fee. To their best memory, this is the only act of kindness the family received from the police. They lived in a slum.

The murder of Sherry Ann Duncan made headlines again almost two years after the three scapegoats were released. The Crime Suppression Division had been reinvestigating the case and on February 6, 1995, they arrested two brothers—Somjai and Somphong Bunyarit—who were believed to be the real killers. Thirteen days later, two more men—Samak Toopbuchakan and Peera Wongwaiwut—were arrested. They were said to be close friends of the Bunyarit brothers.

On November 1, 1995, Suvibol Patpongpanit, a wealthy businesswoman and a former lover of Winai, turned herself in to the police. She was later released on five-million baht bail. She was believed to be the mastermind of the murder and was portrayed as a jealous woman who had been bent on revenge.

The police concluded that Suvibol had hired the men to kill Sherry out of jealousy after she found out that Winai was cheating on her with the young girl. The Bunyarit brothers used to work for Winai and were acquainted with Sherry as they would drive her to school and their wives acted as minders when Winai was busy.

They later fell out with Winai and went to work for Suvibol. Given that they held a grudge against their former boss, the police believed it was easy for Suvibol to persuade them to commit the murder for her.

The police believed that Peera, who was a taxi driver, picked Sherry up from school with Somjai and Somphong. The men somehow persuaded her to get into the taxi, possibly with a ruse regarding Winai. Sherry eventually realised she was not on the usual route and tried to escape but was strangled to death. Then the men dropped her body at the deserted mangrove where the crab-seller couple found her two days later.

The most shocking twist of all was the arrest on January 18, 1996 of Pramern Potplad, the key witness whose testimony had led to four wrongful convictions. He pleaded guilty to perjury and was sentenced to eight years in jail. He told the court that he had been acting under orders from a policeman named Mongkol Sripo, who was in charge of the 1986 investigation into Sherry's murder. [1]

Krasae said Mongkol and another investigator had brought Pramern into a room, shown him their pictures, and told him to identify them as the men he had seen carrying Sherry out of Winai's condominium before she was found dead.

However, Mongkol resigned before he was dismissed by the Royal Thai Police and had already settled in America for several years, thus escaping legal action against him.

The other five investigators who worked on the case with Mongkol were duly promoted at work before reaching retirement. None ever faced criminal action as it was ruled that they had no knowledge of Mongkol's plan to frame the innocent men. While the four scapegoats suffered, these policemen not only were awarded with

---

1   A police fact-finding team determined that Mongkol had hired Pramern to provide false testimony and act as a witness against the four defendants. Mongkol was later dismissed from the police service for serious disciplinary offences with retroactive effect to October 1 1993. The dismissal order was issued in 1999.

unmerited career advancements but also got off scot-free.

One account said Pramern had been paid a pitiful fee of 500 baht to conspire with Mongkol while another claimed he was paid in zinc tiles, which he used to patch the roof of his house. The idea of a 'witness-for-hire' might sound absurd to some but several inmates in Bang Kwang will tell you that some police resort to this 'shortcut' along with embellishments in their reports to make their case relevant to the prosecutors so they can close the case.

The Office of Attorney General held a seminar, which was inspired by the aftermath of the wrongful convictions in the Sherry Ann case, looking at how to provide better protection for innocent people. Suggestions and opinions from this seminar led to changes in judicial procedure and later were included in the constitution.

After Mongkol and Premern had been exposed, the two remaining scapegoats and the families of the deceased men did not receive any apology or help from the police. An uphill struggle to instigate a 54.5 million baht lawsuit for compensation against the six police officers who had framed the four men and the Royal Thai Police began in 1997.

Recalling the day he tried to file the complaint at the Crime Suppression Division, Krasae said, 'No one dared to touch our complaint as the police officers who falsely arrested us had become high-ranking ones by that time. Luckily, the moment I was about to give up and go home

I came across the police officer who had reopened the case and he accepted our complaint.'

Krasae and Thawat and five relatives of the two dead men, became seven plaintiffs in this lawsuit and requested a pro bono trial which would exempt them from having to pay hefty court fees. Krasae said the police tried to buy time from the beginning saying the plaintiffs were not eligible for financial help as they were not really poor people. It took almost three years before the court allowed them a pro bono trial. Afterwards, the proceedings were delayed by many deferments from the police.

Krasae outlined his part of the compensation request as follows: 10 million baht for making him a murderer of a young girl in the public eye; five million baht for the assault by the Samut Prakan police; 96,300 baht for salaries he could have made from his job; another 10 million baht for the hardship he had to endure in the prison including being shackled at all time, poor diet and trauma from being jailed with unstable and dangerous inmates on death row.

He didn't expect to be awarded the 25 million baht but he hoped he would get enough to pay off the debts incurred by his aging mother who had to borrow money to pay for trips she made from Ayutthaya province to visit him at the prison in Nonthaburi.

Meanwhile, almost two years after the round-up of the second set of suspects in Sherry Ann's murder, on August 6, 1997, the court of first instance handed down death penalties to three defendants; Samak, Somphong and Suvibol. Samak pleaded guilty and implicated Suvibol as the mastermind.

In early 1999, the Appeal Court upheld three death sentences but the Supreme Court acquitted Suvibol due to insufficient evidence and commuted the other two death sentences to life in prison on May 29, 1999. Somphong was named as the real killer and Samak his accomplice. Some said they were just more scapegoats.

Thawat succumbed to throat cancer before he could receive closure on the compensation suit. Kittisak, who represented the seven plaintiffs, said he had contacted Pramern to testify against the police while he was in jail and Pramern had agreed to do so. However, due to delays in the legal proceedings, Pramern was released and it took time for the lawyer to locate him again. Kittisak said that a few days before a court hearing at which Pramern was due to appear, his wife and child were arrested for narcotics possession and Pramern disappeared again, this time for good.

About this suspicious disappearance of his key witness against the police, Kittisak said: 'If you ask me, he has obviously been abducted. But I can't say for certain who is his abductor. My theory is that the real culprit or culprits colluded with the police to frame these four innocent men. The police who are responsible for this treachery know who the real culprits are and must have been paid a hefty sum for setting these scapegoats up. No one would agree to take such a risky action, which could completely jeopardise their career, unless the fee was right. Fabricating things in order to make an innocent person look guilty can only be the work of the police. The prosecutors have no part in it.'

Drawing upon the case, Kittisak proposed a practice of at least two separate police teams working on one case to ensure transparency.

It was six years before the Civil Court ruled, on September 25, 2003, that the Royal Thai Police had to pay Krasae and the relatives of the three dead men about 26 million baht in compensation because they had introduced a false witness to frame the four men. Presiding Judge Kanchana said, 'The police, Major Mongkol Sripo in particular, have a legal obligation to uphold the law, but they failed to do so by rigging the investigation. Therefore, they are liable to pay for the damage incurred.' The verdict stipulated the compensation plus accrued 7.5 percent interest dating back to 1997, when the compensation suit had been filed.

Krasae, the sole living scapegoat, was awarded the most with 10 million baht, which was less than half what he had asked for. Thawat, who died before the ruling, was awarded eight million baht and the sum was expected to go to his daughters. Rungchalerm's family was awarded 6.6 million baht while the remaining 1.3 million baht went to Pitak's mother, who said no amount of compensation could make up for the loss of her closest child.

This should have marked an ending to this 17-year-long tragedy but another outcry occurred after the then national police chief Sant Sarutanond said a hasty payment would set a bad precedent. He also said he would ask legal advisers to review the verdict before determining whether to appeal. His statement was deemed to be very insensitive. It was also in contrast to a response to the verdict by then premier Thaksin Shinawatra, who said the police should not delay payment of the compensation further with a lengthy appeal process.

For a time it was uncertain whether the police would appeal. Tun, Rungchalerm's wife, said, 'If you ask me whether I hate the police, the answer is yes. But I also realise that there are good police out there. I want to implore the police not to submit an appeal [against the compensation ruling]. I'm so exhausted. Please allow me closure before I die.'

Tun hoped to move out of the slum they were living in with the 6.6 million baht compensation, fulfilling a long overdue dream of her dead husband of a better life for his family. Krasae also pleaded with the police not to appeal.

On October 1, 2003, the seven plaintiffs handed a petition to Prime Minister Thaksin Shinawatra, pleading with the Royal Thai Police not to appeal the ruling. During his weekly radio programme on October 4, 2003, Thaksin expressed his sympathy for the men. The plaintiffs had been through a terrible ordeal, he said, and the court had already ruled that the police were guilty so the police should immediately compensate them out of their own pocket. Their superiors should pay close attention to how their subordinates conducted themselves, to prevent them from taking bribes or engaging in other sorts of corruption, he added. He instructed the secretary to the Cabinet to tell the Royal Police and Attorney General's office not to appeal. The police later confirmed they would not appeal.

In the same year, the Justice Ministry paid 13 million baht in compensation to the first group of 21 crime victims and 31 wrongfully prosecuted people under the Constitution and Criminal Victims Compensation Act which guarantees the right to compensation from the state for victims of wrongful prosecution and crime victims. At that time, 540 people had filed complaints demanding compensation.

Among those were a couple who had been detained for four years from 1998 on charges of robbing and attempting to murder a customer at their own restaurant. They received about 560,000 baht, which went to pay off debts they had incurred from hiring lawyers to defend their innocence. They said the sum was not worth their loss of freedom.

Another wrongfully prosecuted man named Krit was compensated with a sum of 856,600 baht. His mistress became furious with him when he would not divorce his legal wife to be with her. She conspired with police relatives to frame him for rape and robbery. The Criminal and Appeal Court found him guilty.

During his five years and nine months in Ayutthaya prison, he studied law and defended himself in the

Supreme Court and won the case. Krit suggested that the state should imprison the investigators who wronged him instead of compensating him.

The figures speak for themselves. From a database at the Office of Rights and Freedom at the Justice Ministry, out of 610 cases that came before the courts in 2005, complaints of wrongful indictment were received in 355 cases. For 214 of these cases, 60 million baht was paid in compensation. During the first nine months of 2006, out of 354 complaints of wrongful indictment, 216 of them were compensated with a combined 58 million baht.

Despite the sheer amount of injustice in the Sherry Ann Duncan case, I believe legacies remain that have lead to improvements in the Thai judicial system. At the very least, the police reopened the case and rectified the miscarriage of justice.

The harshest criticism of the Thai criminal justice system is reserved for the police force, which is viewed as incompetent and corrupt. The headlines about bad police never fail to shock and upset the public yet not a year goes by without talk of reform in the police force or another scandal. This is not to say that all police officers are corrupt and unethical in their conduct. To a degree, I can sympathise with good policemen who are discouraged by the unfavourable opinion of them that many people have, as prison guards are viewed as violent and corrupt too.

I've met killers who showed no remorse, boasting about the number of people they killed minutes before their execution. On those unfortunate occasions, I couldn't help but feel grateful that the police arrested these psychopaths, making Thailand a safer place. I would like to believe that, with pressure and the watchful eyes of the media and concerned citizens, the police force would not allow a case like the murder of Sherry Ann to happen again.

Chapter 7 ❧

WHAT LIFE AFTER PRISON?

Many inmates in the Bangkok Hilton are adamant that they are victims of a crime rather than the perpetrators. They insist they were tortured by policemen until they confessed to bogus charges. It is unnerving to think that some officers, who are the first line of justice, could be wrongdoers themselves. Yet even today there is still one report after another of police who have behaved thuggishly.

In my role as a prison guard, I paid little attention to most of these self-proclaimed fall guys. That changed when news of a group of border patrol police who framed people for possession of narcotics made headlines in early 2008.

The police group in question, led by police captain Nat Chonnithiwanit, abducted people, physically abused them, extorted money from them, forced them to participate in undercover stings and charged them with drug offences. About 200 drug cases instigated by them were to be reinvestigated.

In December 2009, Nat and seven co-defendants were found guilty of extorting a 300,000 baht ransom from a woman they had abducted. They also threatened to charge her with having 800 pills of *yaba* (amphetamine). Each of them was sentenced to five years in jail and ordered to pay damages to her. At the time of writing, they are facing about 30 cases in all.

The scandal seemed to echo the story told by Pitak, who had done time in Bang Kwang. Pitak and his former lover Nok had been convicted of possession of heroin with intent to sell when they were a young couple. Each was sentenced to life in prison for a crime they insisted they hadn't committed.

I visited Pitak and Nok to ask them about their story. You are free to make your own judgment. This is what Pitak said to me:

When children are being unruly, some parents warn them to behave by saying: 'I'll call the police to come and get you.' To many Thais, the police are not only figures of authority but also of fear and disdain. To me, this notion is justified.

I used to work at a pier management company in the southern province of Trang. Fishing and transport boats operating in the Andaman Sea visited our pier for maintenance and repair. I wore two hats as a manager and head mechanic. Life was good to me then but my family hadn't always had it easy.

During World War II, the Japanese soldiers arrived on a beach in Songkla in December 1941. My father co-owned a small factory and one day while driving a truck alone, he was ambushed by Japanese soldiers. They demanded the truck at gunpoint and forced him to work for them as a repairman. After the war was over, he was reunited with Mae. Although Por and Mae were neither highly educated nor rich, they always taught me to work hard towards my goals by being examples themselves.

So I did and by 1982 I had many friends and a steady well-paid job. One thing was still missing from my life: romance. Then I met Nok, who is of Hainan Chinese descent. She worked at a coffee shop in the city area of Trang. It belonged to her uncle and was one of many businesses her wealthy family owned. Although I was very busy at work, I couldn't help but go to the shop more to get to know her. The 20 kilometres between my place and the coffee shop wasn't a problem as I had a company car.

Years of being schooled in Bangkok made her more refined, chatty and sociable than the girls I had been used to. Although a *sao krung* (city girl) like her attracted admirers like bees to a flower, I had the edge in the form of company car.

When we were in the mood for a fun-filled night out, we went to Hat Yai in Songkla, the nearest place for such entertainment then. Nok and I communicated openly and we talked about the deeper things, including the fact that she had run away from a cheating husband in Bangkok. She had moved to Trang to think over her unhappy marriage. I knew she was on the rebound and might not take me seriously but I was glad to be with her nonetheless. We weren't conservative and it didn't take long before we were intimate.

One day I noticed she was preoccupied and asked what was bothering her. After a long silence, she said, 'I'm not sure how to break it to you... Mong has been trying to persuade me to hold drugs for him and to pass them to his buyer.'

Mong was an acquaintance of ours from the coffee shop. He wasn't fluent in Thai but I'm not sure of his origins. I knew him as a seller of cosmetics and clothing, which fashionable Nok bought regularly. She had also agreed to sell clothes for him at her uncle's shop and the business was doing well.

She continued, 'Of course, I said "no" but he is persistent. I fear repercussion if I continue to say no. I still have my dealings with him and I'm not sure what to do.'

I suggested she distance herself from him and let her relatives handle business with him instead. We never discussed it again.

That was when I found out he was a drug dealer but the revelation wasn't a big shock to me. The smuggling of oil, rice, sugar and mineral rocks by boat was rife, among other vices, in Trang. I was privy to these illicit deals because of my work but I wasn't interested in joining their ranks or playing informer for fear of retaliation. At one time, a man who claimed to be in charge of the entire smuggling ring had tried to persuade me to facilitate his business at the pier in exchange for a huge sum.

He said, 'One call to my army friend is all it takes to solve every problem you might have with the police.' He handed me the business card of a high-ranking army officer. I returned it and declined his offer as politely as I could, saying I already had enough on my plate. For all I know, he might have been bluffing.

The company I worked for ordered water tanks from a factory in Hat Yai. We advanced a cheque to the factory owner in June but by September still hadn't received the order. I was asked to sort it out and decided to kill two birds with one stone: visit the factory and have a weekend with Nok in Hat Yai. Before we left Trang, Nok told me she was pregnant and I took the news as a good omen despite our affair. Little did we know that it would be the last weekend we would have to celebrate.

When we got there, the factory owner was away on business. His wife called him and said he would surely be back later and would meet me at my hotel the following morning. I checked into the hotel on Saturday, September 11, 1982. There was no sign of him on Sunday morning and I thought that either he was late or he had decided to stand me up. I went to reception to pay for the room while Nok waited on a sofa at the other side of the lobby. While I was checking out, I heard footsteps approaching me from behind. Before I could turn to face them, my wrists were grabbed and forced against my back. Handcuffed, I struggled to break free but there was very little I could do against the force of three strange men. The receptionist looked on in shock.

My heart sank further when I heard Nok cry for help. We were forced to walk in different directions. They pushed and shoved me to the car park where I was told to get into a black pick-up truck. My first thought was that they were kidnappers, because Nok's family was rich, and I was being taken along as a bonus.

Blindfolded, I tried to remain calm but the darkness intensified my fear. Sweat ran down my face as hands pressed hard on both of my shoulders. I knew it was still daytime but I didn't shout for help for fear of being beaten or killed. The abductors remained silent all the way. Finally, the truck came to a stop and the blindfold was removed. They manhandled me into a deserted hut in the middle of a rubber plantation and sat me on the floor, propped up against a wall.

One of the abductors, whom I later knew as Amnat, said, 'We are plainclothes police officers and now you are in a property of an anti-drug agency.'

I was too dumbstruck to say anything back. Another man quickly brought out a bag full of white powder and a scale. He weighed the bag in front of me while the other took photographs of what was happening. Their movements were swift and in sync as if they had done this many times before. Amnat produced a piece of paper and told me to sign it. The moment my mind registered what was written on it, I was jolted out of confusion. It was a fabricated arrest report that said I had been found with heroin.

'What the hell is going on? Why did you bring me here?' I demanded.

Amnat, who was clearly the one in charge, said, 'Just sign the damn thing and you'll be sent to a police station or else...'

I replied, 'I don't know what's in the bag but it's certainly not mine. Why are you doing this to me?'

Instead of an answer he tapped at a pistol tucked into the pocket of his trousers. I didn't need further persuasion. I learnt that Nok had given in as easily as I had. What else could we do?

On the way to the police station, I hoped the officers there would listen to me and believe that Nok and I had been framed. But, as a Thai proverb goes, we ran away from a tiger only to face a crocodile. The worst had yet to befall us. The clock said one hour before midnight when I was thrown into a holding cell. Within a few hours, my life had been turned upside down. There in the cell, I experienced some of the most confusing and desperate moments of my life.

An hour later I was taken out of the cell and into another room in the police station. I knew what was about to happen and felt so helpless. I was told to sign a blank piece of paper, which I was told would be my interrogation report. I said 'no' and within seconds I felt hard blows on my face. After having a go at me, they got creative. They stacked up chairs in a pile and forced me to stand on top of it. Together they kicked the stack so it would tumble down and my body would hit the floor. They laughed like children engaging in mischievous play. All the while, they lied that Nok, who was being kept in another cell, had already confessed to the crime. There were other forms of assault, including punches to my stomach and slaps to my face, but I don't want to elaborate. Suffice to say that I didn't sustain any permanent injury and I count myself among the fortunate ones. I somehow managed to endure the pain and refused to sign the paper they thrust upon me. The second night they took me out of the cell and subjected me to the same routine.

While Nok and I were on remand, our families were propositioned by several police officers, offering help in an exchange for hefty fees. They claimed they could use their connections with court officials either to guarantee bail would be granted or even to rig the court ruling in our favour. They were like vultures trying to pick shreds of meat from a dying animal. They seemed to work independently so I didn't know who to trust. Even if I could somehow produce the money they demanded, there was no guarantee they would fulfill their promises. Nok's family, however, spent a fortune on them.

Corrupt police officers continued to pressure me to sign the interrogation report but I refused to sign away my life. Obviously, they could put anything in it. When I thought they couldn't go any lower, a man I remembered as one of the six abductors visited me. He said they could secure bail release for Nok and me if we helped them to catch two more people. He didn't explain exactly what was required so I assumed they wanted us to act as bait to lure people into drug-buying stings while we were on bail. I had had enough of their callousness and said, 'You scum, just leave me alone.' He shrugged off my insult and said, 'You'll be sorry. Definitely will.'

At this point, Nok and I hadn't been in contact with each other since the abduction and trust between us waned. My relatives started to feed me stories that Nok was involved in the drug trade while hers were pinning the blame on me. My family accused me of being infatuated with Nok when I defended her innocence but saying she was a drug dealer didn't make sense. Nok's family is wealthy and she worked for a firm on Bangkok's affluent Silom Road before she got married. It didn't add up.

Nok admitted to her family that she was three months pregnant. A child conceived outside wedlock when she already had a husband made our affair an utter disgrace. They scorned me for corrupting her.

My relatives urged me to sign the blank paper which was to contain the interrogation report. If I didn't, they said the police would not process our bail requests. I finally gave in, however, to the emotional pleas of Nok's mother on condition that she stop trying to persuade Nok to abort our unborn child. Nhe, Nok's grandmother, was planning to hire a guard to smuggle in medication to Nok that could cause a miscarriage. Nhe believed the unborn child was a *tua suai* (jinx) which was bringing Nok great misfortune and by getting rid of it she would be freed.

I can only wonder now how different things might have been if both sides had got together and put our lawyers to work building our defence. However, given how ineffective our lawyers were, I don't think it would have mattered. My family hired a lawyer through recommendation but he turned out to be a huge disappointment. He rarely visited me to discuss my defence and the one time he did he offended me greatly with a suggestion that he would compose my testimony to be in line with the police fabrication.

'How can you represent me when you don't even believe me?' I demanded.

He replied: 'It doesn't matter what actually happened as it would be your word against theirs and whose words do you think the court will buy? Pointing out discrepancies in their report is your best chance. Or better yet you should plead guilty and get a smaller sentence.'

Given that I had already and regrettably signed the falsified interrogation report, I agreed to see what he could write for me.

Nok's lawyer recommended that she plead guilty, adding that 25 years in jail would be the worst-case scenario. Her relatives, however, detested the idea of having the family name tainted by a conviction and insisted she fight the case and declare her innocence or else she would never see them again.

Our families and friends eventually gathered enough money and land deeds worth a few hundred thousand baht to meet the collateral demanded for our bail applications. However, we were denied bail as the charges against us were considered high priority and because the police in charge of the case objected. The court ordered that Nok be escorted to a hospital when she went into labour. I was to be tried as defendant number one, Nok number two.

My lawyer continued to be very unprofessional. He gave me the scripted testimony an hour before I had to appear before the judge. I was told to memorise it and recite as much as I could. I blew my lid. 'Are you kidding me? This is not a play and I'm not an actor. I will testify with the truth!' I said. It dawned on me then that he might have been working with the police all along. Nok refused to acknowledge my existence. I didn't know at the time that it was a part of her defence.

Amnat must have been moonlighting as an actor because he 'recalled' before the court a very long fabricated story in great detail. 'Your honour, an informant reported that the two suspects were looking for a buyer of 3.5 kilogrammes of heroin for 900,000 baht. I decided an undercover sting was the best way to expose them. I assigned another informant to play buyer and an officer to play his bodyguard. They went to a hotel in Trang to conduct the first sting on August 29.

'The female suspect was waiting in the hotel restaurant when they arrived. She counted the cash, which had been borrowed from a US anti-drug agency, before excusing herself to phone the male suspect whom she told to bring the heroin. She came back to say that she couldn't contact him and postponed the deal to September 2. They went to the same hotel the second time and met both suspects, who led them to room 423. There both suspects counted the money, gave it back and told them to wait at the same table on the ground floor.

'The male suspect went out to get the drugs but came back to call off the deal, saying he had spotted a policeman in plain clothing walking in front of the house where he kept the drugs. He suggested a new place to meet, which is the hotel in Hat Yai where we conducted the third sting and arrested them on September 12.

'I ordered five police officers to assume disguises to observe the sting, which was arranged to take place in the hotel car park. The female suspect got into our pick-up truck and counted the money while we were waiting for the male suspect to arrive. He stopped his black pick-up truck near ours and came out with a brown bag in his arms. The officer who played the bodyguard greeted him and checked the substance in the bag. He then touched his hair repeatedly to signal the team to arrest both suspects.'

Nok unexpectedly stood up and tearfully shouted at Amnat: 'You liar. You lying bastard!' Her lawyer told her that that kind of language was unacceptable in court and asked her to compose herself. I wanted to punch Amnat to a pulp for the lies he spewed. I made do with writing his name under my feet and squashing it against the floor as if it were a cockroach.

Nok testified with a story her lawyer had made up. Clearly upset, she delivered it unconvincingly.

'On September 12, my friends and I went to see an underwriter in Hat Yai to buy a life policy from him but he was away. We decided to walk around the town before returning home. It was about 30 minutes before midnight when a white pick-up truck stopped in front of me. Three men who claimed to be plainclothes police officers told me I must go with them. I was taken to a property they claimed was owned by an anti-drug agency. There I was forced to sign papers that I didn't read because I was so traumatised. I haven't met defendant number one before in my life.'

To back up the lie that I was a stranger to her, she presented pictures of her wedding. She said she had been married for two years before she came to Trang to nurse her older cousin who had become paralysed.

Unlike Nok, I decided to tell the presiding judge what really had happened but he looked unimpressed. Perhaps our contradictory stories drove the nails deeper into our coffins but I wasn't aware of this. I was in my prisoner uniform, feeling intimidated by the system that assumed I was guilty until proven innocent. My morale was at a low ebb due to months of being on remand and infrequent visits from my lawyer who wanted me to lie in my testimony. I realised my chances of convincing the judge of my innocence were as good as winning first prize in the lottery.

My lawyer's words rang in my mind as I sat down: '... it would be your word against theirs and whose words do you think the court will buy?'

The presiding judge took Amnat at his word and believed the three buying stings had taken place. He ruled that Amnat and the other five officers had no motive to frame us since we hadn't known each other before the arrest. I wonder how much a hitman knows about his target before he pulls the trigger. The falsified interrogation and arrest reports were brought up as solid evidence against us.

In them, both of us 'admitted' to keeping the brown bag for Mong, who asked us to pass it to someone in Hat Yai, but not to knowing what was in it. The judge said it was unconvincing for us to agree to carry something not knowing what was in it in the first place. How could it make sense when the police were liars? Testimonies given by two witnesses of Nok and four of mine failed to carry any weight in our favour.

The judge went on to say that it was unconvincing that I, as a man of as many responsibilities as I claimed, would choose to stay overnight at the hotel to sort things out with the factory owner when I should have returned to my company where bigger jobs awaited. Nok's claim of being away from her husband to nurse an ill cousin was also dismissed.

We were sentenced to life in prison on December 30, 1983, almost 16 months after we had been abducted. It took that long before the first court read its verdict because there were many witnesses involved and several deferments caused by the police's side.

Upon hearing the verdict, I immediately felt the will to live was taken out of me. I was overwhelmed by distress while Nok sobbed hard. It was heartbreaking to see her in that state. We exchanged a gaze as if to convey to each other 'how could they do this to us?'. She shook her head in disbelief as her sobs became louder. I had to look away as I was nearly in tears.

In my opinion, it is just a fact of life that, in Thailand, rogue policemen can force you to admit to any crime, especially if you are poor and uneducated. I'm certain of this as I have lived it. Nok and I had some resources and education but look what we were reduced to. I met several drug suspects while on remand who all claimed they had been made scapegoats by the same group of people. We bonded over the common resentment we had towards them and shared theories on why they preyed on us.

Our consensus was that they wanted to impress their superiors with how effective they were in the hope of securing big promotions and making money from drug cases. To them, we were just scores. My fellow scapegoats said that they used small-time drug dealers to work for them. Some claimed their wives had been coerced into sleeping with the police.

Before the first court's ruling, Nok was escorted by two guards to the hospital to deliver our baby. She was allowed to stay there for only one night because a female prisoner had escaped through a window after giving birth leaving her baby behind. We named our baby girl Pin.

I was transferred to Bang Kwang, Nok and Pin to Lard Yao. Pin was about eight months old at that time. There were about 30 infants being raised behind bars.

Nhe took Pin's time of birth to a fortune-teller who said she was an auspicious child. She gladly informed

Nok: 'Your child is a blessing. If it wasn't for her, the master said you would be dead already.' She offered to raise Pin for us. Nok was certain that she could trust Pin with her now. I feared that Nhe would raise her out of obligation but not well, because she was not a legitimate grandchild and Nhe had considered her a jinx initially.

Nok raised Pin inside the prison until she was three. After that children start to form memories and no one wants them to have prison as their first recollection. Pin wasn't crying too much when they had to part as Nok had been telling her of what was to come all along. It was Nok who was inconsolable afterwards because she derived so much joy from rearing her baby girl. Had she not decided to give up Pin to Nhe, our little girl would have been sent to a Christian orphanage in Chonburi and any chance of them reuniting would have been diminished. Nhe proved me wrong as she grew to love Pin so much. I can't thank her enough for raising Pin for us and arranging for her to see us during contact visits over the years.

I had been in Songkla prison before so I was somewhat prepared for the notorious Bang Kwang. Feeling numb about life in general also helped. Boasts about body count by murderers and gunmen no longer startled me. Neither did their tattoos of big tigers or dragons. However, it was still very difficult for me, as an innocent man, to live in the prison. Conversation between the real criminals was often about people they knew from the same circles. After they realised I didn't really know any of the names they were dropping, they assumed that I was snitching on them.

I wasn't subjected to a *rab nong* (orientation) when I first arrived at Bang Kwang. By orientation, I mean newcomers being physically abused by those who were jailed before them. I consider myself very fortunate in this regard as this kind of practice exists even now, especially in provincial prisons.

Four women claim their relatives were attacked and killed by other inmates at a prison in Kanchanaburi on December 31, 2009. The four men had been transferred from another prison with 34 others, all of whom were beaten up by prisoners who said it was how they 'welcomed' newcomers. Apparently one man died on the spot while the rest were seriously injured. A 29-year-old drug offender with four months left to serve died after being beaten up and stabbed in the neck and all over his body.

I first saw addicts queuing to shoot up in Bang Kwang. Heroin was dissolved in a spoon and they eagerly tapped their arms to make their veins become clearer. All shared one tube with a needle at one end. One by one, they sucked the liquid from the spoon into the tube, stabbed the needle, sucked the tube lightly to make sure that blood was going up it and blew hard to push the liquid into their bodies. Some addicts claimed their relatives secretly gave them some drugs when they had to go to court, which they would use immediately so they wouldn't be caught later.

Many young men were forced to become *nong* by convicts who held knives against their necks as they raped them. Others woke up in pain and bleeding because they had been drugged and violated in their sleep. The more fortunate ones met suitors who offered food and friendship until they felt indebted to them and eventually conceded to their sexual advances, knowing they would be provided for. I didn't mind the lovebirds much except for when they noisily quarrelled because the 'wife' in the relationship was denying the 'husband' a pleasure unless he paid first.

It is disgusting what inmates do to kill time in Bang Kwang. Some inject lubricant from factories into their testicles to enlarge their manhood. They have to be sent to the hospital later because these botched 'enhancements' often go awfully wrong.

The inmates have ample opportunity to sharpen their skills as criminals if they wish. Given the vast network of contacts, after their release they can find a job in the underworld through recommendation as well. No doubt some left the Big Tiger worse people than when they walked in. Those who started out as robbers either became burglars or drug dealers. Knife wielders took up explosives or firearms.

At the other extreme, many have put their minds to education, religion, music and occupational training. A former soldier named Manote completed a few bachelor degrees while he served time in Bang Kwang. Like me, he had been wrongly convicted of drug dealing. Before being jailed, he had lived and worked in the Inkayut army base in southern Pattani province where he helped his wife to run a small food stall in his spare time.

Sombat, a known supplier of stolen cars in the province, used to stop by to eat there often because many of his buyers were army guys. The men became good friends. One day Sombat was pulled over by a few police officers who found heroin hidden in his car while Manote was with him. Both were arrested and Manote was jailed because he happened to be with a real drug dealer.

Armed with few degrees, he set out to find a decent job in Bangkok but his qualifications couldn't outweigh his conviction. The last I heard, he had gone to Phuket to stay with his cousins and mind a fruit stand for them there.

By and large, Bang Kwang functions like a school for criminals. On top of that, it is like a drug expo of sorts given that major dealers from different countries have landed themselves in there. News about drug busts never fails to generate talk in the prison. Some crack their knuckles in anticipation of settling scores with the newcomers for unpaid drug bills or other reasons.

One drug dealer named Khong, who had been known to work for the police in many buying stings, received a very brutal welcome—an overnight beating up by some men he had helped the police to catch. I still remember his pleas for mercy while his assailants laughed and howled as they kicked and punched him senseless.

'This is what you get for putting me in this hell hole,' one man roared before dealing a kick to his stomach while he was lying on his side. The impact prompted him to curl up in the foetal position and cough up a small amount of blood. The malicious 'orientation' unfolded in the cell opposite mine. I shut my eyes tight and hoped the night would go quickly. I figured his attackers had arranged to be in the same cell with him. His cries were loud enough to reach the night shift guards but none came to his rescue. He survived but was maimed for life. He had worked for the police for too long and perhaps knew so much that they wanted to get rid of him one way or another.

Fellow inmates agreed with me that violence is common in the local prisons while the central ones like Klong Prem or Bang Kwang are more about illicit businesses.

Each cell was overcrowded. I shared one cell with about 20 men. The most coveted spot was the corner farthest from the open squatting toilet. The cost of this spot varied from 1,000 to 2,000 baht. When the gamblers wanted to stay up and play, they rented space from cellmates so they could put down their mats.

Whenever I got up to pee during the night, I forfeited my sleep space because a cellmate sleeping next to me would roll into it. We slept like one condensed mass ready to expand when space became available. Sometimes we all had to sleep on our sides simply because there was not enough room. When I finished peeing, I had to ask cellmates to move or shove them away to get my space back. Disturbed from their sleep, some picked fights with me.

I spent many nights, tossing and turning on the floor because the weather was too hot and the light was on all the time. Once I was unfortunate enough to sleep opposite the toilet while a cellmate was taking a dump. He was urinating at the same time and he 'sprayed' a little bit on my feet. We ended up having a fist fight.

Inmates with business acumen make money through various ventures such as loan-sharking, gambling and lotteries. Each of us was allowed to use up to 200 baht in coupons a day but I saw many freely using cash. Although I didn't know how much cash was being smuggled into Bang Kwang, I reckon it must be in the millions, given that heavy gamblers incurred hundreds of thousands of baht in debt. Gamblers who were on a losing streak had to come up with money quickly or else they would feel the house's wrath when 'samurais' were paid to beat or stab them. Most of the samurai were drug addicts and dealers who would take any dirty job for money to fund their addiction. They usually worked for the drug lords in Bang Kwang.

These drug lords could conduct their business with ease, especially when their merchandise was being sent in on the back of a *singha* (lion) or prison guard. They use this nickname for guards because the symbol of the Corrections Department is a male deity riding a lion.

The gangs in charge of their respective buildings collect money from the operators of illegal businesses to bribe the guards who, in return, tell them in advance when the next raid will take place so all trace of illegal activities and prohibited items are hidden away. However, my treasured collection of clippings on miscarriages of justice was seized and burnt during a raid as the authorities feared that I would use the information against the prison. I had hoped to use them to raise awareness of flaws in the justice system.

Whenever the guards pushed lock-up time back by one hour, I knew there would be an execution that day. In the sleeping quarters, just a wire mesh in the middle separated the cells of death row inmates from the others. I saw what happened on the other side when prison guards came to pick up inmates who would soon be shot dead. It must be torture for them to be fettered all the time. Toilets in their cells broke because they accidentally dropped their shackles on them time after time. That says something about how heavy the chains are.

They had different ways to distract themselves from thinking about their impending doom: meditation, study, music or drugs. Few I met accepted their fate or appeared to be willing to die.

I remember a serial rapist-murderer who proclaimed while being collected, 'I killed four and they get only one (pointing at himself) so I win.' He startled me with his absence of remorse as he cockily walked to his death.

Many buckled from fear so much they couldn't walk properly. On my side of the quarters, there were those who placed bets on who would go next. They followed the progress of death row cases through the grapevine.

Those convicted of serious charges or repeat offenders were unlikely to be spared.

While I had to fight off evils and temptations around me, an inner hell was brewing. The bitterness I felt from the injustice of my situation and being disowned by friends and family consumed me. The longer I spent behind bars, the less frequent their visits became. My relatives resented me for bringing shame on the family name while friends wanted nothing to do with me for fear the police would suspect they were drug dealers.

My immediate family lived in Trang, some 800km from the prison, so I couldn't blame them for not visiting me enough. I couldn't help but pity myself though when I saw the families of foreigners who flew across oceans to meet their sons. No guards ever demanded money from me. The fact that I rarely received visitors told them I didn't have a baht to spare.

Gradually I channelled my energy from grieving into my own survival. Inmates in my position usually either become servants to drug lords or resort to dishonest means to line their own pockets. I opted to make others feel indebted to me by doing them favours and, in return, I lived on their tokens of gratitude. I taught the Thai language to hill tribe people from the north, young Muslims whose mother tongue is Yawa as well as several Nigerians. I was assigned to escort inmates who were called out to see visitors. I built friendships with them and they kindly gave me some leftovers, as did the guards who noticed that I was trying to make myself useful. The inmates I met were not all evil—well, not all the time at least. They knew how to be grateful and a giver when they were shown kindness first. I also played a pivotal role in a campaign to raise the literacy rate among the prisoners through non-formal education.

My track record eventually earned me a 'job' at the prison hospital. There I took care of patients and assisted the doctor in performing minor medical procedures. It was safer there than an ordinary ward. The downside was the strong smell of disinfectant and the sight of dying patients. I never really got used to that.

Many times I stepped on puddles of faeces and urine left by terminally ill patients who had lost bladder control among other bodily and mental functions. They went back and forth between Jekyll and Hyde. During lucid moments, they thanked the doctors and me profusely for our care. They poured out to us how bitter they felt at being forgotten. In moments of great pain, they threw tantrums and became very aggressive towards us. Some suffered so much, they cursed everyone until the last minutes of their lives as they faded into oblivion. Seeing how people decayed physically and mentally was deeply saddening.

Mentally unstable inmates were put in a separate section. Some of them liked to cut their own stomachs or arms or randomly attack people. The really aggressive ones were chained to building columns when the section was full.

When I felt like I was about to lose my mind, I talked to the doctor. Our sessions fell into a routine of me retelling my ordeal and him being condescending and giving me strong medicine. He said, 'You may be innocent, as you insist, but can you be sure about what you did in your past life? You might have been a drug dealer who got away back then and karma is making you pay now.'

I stopped seeing him eventually. I was sick of the way he dealt with me. His drugs also made me feel drowsy. In hindsight, he probably thought of me as another nut and, therefore, not to be taken seriously.

I was there when riots broke out in Bang Kwang. I can't get out of my head images of an inmate who was shot dead in the face with his left eye hanging out of its socket or the body of a man beaten to death who turned grotesquely purple. I also remember putting bloody and bruised bodies into coffins or bags with my bare hands. They are not my worst nightmares, however.

The worst come from seeing the guards beat up wounded rioters even as they lay defenseless on the hospital beds. They behaved like barbaric hunters going after their helpless prey while yelling profanities. The rioters pleaded for mercy by putting their hands in prayer and *waied* them but the guards were after blood. The doctor in charge that day was disgusted by them as was I, but we were too afraid to try to stop them. The rioters were left in worse condition than when they had been carried in and the doctors and I had to clean up the mess. We knew they were troublemakers but they didn't deserve to be attacked like that.

Many times I had to sleep in the same room as a corpse or two because nobody came to pick up the deceased at weekends or during long holidays. The cloths that covered them couldn't prevent the strong smell that filled the room. When the guards wanted to collect fingerprints from the bodies for their records, I was ordered to massage and pry open the clutched hands of the dead.

AIDS has claimed many lives there too. It spread through sexual contact and shared needles. Back then inmates died of cholera too, which could have been prevented if clean water had been available. Deaths as a result of murders or fights rarely happened. Some say if you are overexposed to scenes of cruelty, suffering or things that would normally make you cringe, you become desensitized to them. I disagree.

The depressing air of the hospital made me think about what I could look forward to in my own life. Pin was in regular contact over the years but no amount of meaningful conversation during her visits could qualify me as her father. Nok kept in touch with me by letter but our correspondence became infrequent. The only purpose in life I had was to build the family that I should have done 20 years before. I owed Pin two parents. She was already a grown woman but I hoped it was better late than never.

The Supreme Court carried out a verification of the hotel where Amnat claimed the first two undercover stings took place. It turned out neither room 423, where he said Nok and I counted banknotes, nor the restaurant where he said his men met us existed. The High Court ruled there was not enough evidence to support the existence of the first two buying stings. When it came to the third one, however, it ruled that it had happened as described in the arrest reports Nok and I had signed. The same sentence was upheld for both of us. The case was finalised in November 1986.

Our sentence was commuted to 40 years by a mass royal pardon. Nok and I received second cuts in our sentences through individual royal pardons. Now we each had four years left. By 2003, we would be eligible for parole.

I asked the guard in charge of the building I was in to help me with my parole application but he refused saying that as a drug offender I was not entitled to it. I argued that I had been denied equal treatment in sentence reduction from the beginning and my fate was up to the parole commission to decide, not him.

In a letter written on my behalf by my daughter, I summarised my case and stated that I was eligible for parole. I dictated the gist of the letter to Pin over weeks of visits. Later, I was told a letter from the prime minister's office was sent to the Corrections Department, asking about my parole. A few prison officials came and asked me what I had done but I denied having any knowledge of the letter. I was eventually granted parole in 2003.

In my experience, drug offenders have either been excluded from mass pardon or are given smaller sentence reductions than other prisoners. Many of those who were jailed after me got out before I did. A drug dealer is more despicable than a murderer or a rapist, I suppose. I had it worse than anyone because I served time for a crime I didn't commit.

Don't get me wrong, I agree that the severity of the punishment should be in proportion to the crime but giving criminals a chance to get out and redeem themselves is equally important. I'm not sure the lawmakers see it that way. There are those who are the personification of evil in Bang Kwang but there are those who don't deserve to be there too. Two decades behind bars is interminable. How can anyone expect a person to start over after serving that length of time?

I walked out with nothing much. Most of my belongings had been either confiscated or lost. My fellow inmates contributed to my 'departure fund'. Several who owed me fees for writing petitions for royal pardons finally coughed up.

Sitting on a kerb, I shivered under the midday sun. It was 2003 and finally the Big Tiger had released what was left of me from its fangs but I was so damaged I couldn't feel any joy at all. At an age when I should have been planning my retirement, I was starting from scratch— and with very bleak prospects. I felt utterly hopeless and just wanted to vanish. My mind was engulfed by worries about the future. My biggest fear was that I would become an old person who depended on others for survival. My punishment had not ended.

Things were not as bad as they seemed, however. A prison guard offered me a room in his house for a while and helped me to find a cheap place later. I got a job almost right away when a fellow inmate recommended me for a job as a clerk in one his cousin's language schools.

I was released at the time of the War on Drugs launched by former premier Thaksin Shinawatra. It resulted in the deaths of more than 2,200 drug suspects during its first two months, so you could understand why I was anxious. Given my conviction, I feared a policeman would pick me off the street and charge me with another bogus drug offence. Or they could just shoot me dead and blame it on self-defence during a gunfight so they could add one more to the scoreboard. I don't think I was being paranoid given my experience with the police and the fact that they stood to be rewarded with three baht for each *yaba* pill they 'confiscated'. I decided to live on the outskirts of Bangkok, where things are quieter and cheaper.

At our reunion, Pin said I looked even thinner than the last time we met. I wasted no time and asked her to live with me, telling her I would support her through higher education. She agreed and said goodbye to Nhe and her uncle Athit, who always introduced her as one of his own. Her childhood friends don't know that Nok and I are her biological parents. Besides always wearing hand-me-downs, Pin said she had a normal childhood and had no recollection of her time behind bars.

The next step was to get Nok out. I visited her to ask if she wanted my help in getting parole. We were co-defendants and had received the same sentence reductions so she was eligible for parole. It turned out she wasn't aware of her entitlement and didn't even seem to care.

She said, 'How's life on the outside a better choice for me? I'm too old to start over. Here, at least, I have food and a roof over my head. I've lived here this long, so I don't mind more. Please just let me be.'

When I told her that Pin lived with me and that she was more than welcome to join us, her face showed she was having second thoughts.

Nok and I kept in touch through letters but our correspondence gradually became infrequent. I wanted to ask her how she got by but the rules at her prison prohibited her from telling me. She wasn't allowed to talk about what was going on there. She claimed later she couldn't even tell me that life in there was bearable and she watched lot of TV to kill time. It took about a month for her letters to reach me as letter screening and writing rules are taken seriously at her prison.

After she was released on parole, I learnt that she went to stay at a temple in Nonthaburi and entered the monastic life. I thought she wanted to live the rest of her life there to offset her bad karma. She eventually decided to join us and maintain her spirituality through praying and meditation. I know she didn't want to miss out on a chance to be with her daughter.

Living together as a family turned out to be a difficult transition for the three of us. Nok and I fought a lot during the first few months. I guess it was because we felt estranged from each other. Nok is not the woman I used to know and love and I'm sure she feels the same way about me. Anyone jailed for as long as we were surely would come out impaired in some way.

Things are better now. The relationship between Nok and me is platonic and we agree that it's the best way for us to be together. Pin and I work while Nok does some household chores. Nok enjoys her morning routine of selecting an outfit for Pin very much and Pin likes to snuggle on her mother's lap sometimes. I guess we can pass for an ordinary family of three.

When talking to other people, I am sometimes bothered by thoughts that I might do or say something inappropriate or expose my past. Nok doesn't talk much about what she has been through but her keeping quiet about it is a form of remembering.

Apparently she wholeheartedly believes her 20 years in jail were justified and brought on by a transgression she had committed in her past life—the same nonsense that that doctor told me. For me, using karma to justify our ordeal is absurd. Amnat and his team framed us and we each wasted the prime years of our lives because of them. It is that simple.

Nok is still adjusting, coping with irrational anxiety and forgetfulness. She can't be outside late at night and rarely leaves the house on her own. We tried to fix this once with a stroll at a Tesco-Lotus store one evening. At about 9pm, she suddenly pleaded with me in tears to take her home or else something bad would happen to her. Pin and I looked at each other in confusion but we obliged to avoid making a scene.

Signs of her problems became evident a long time ago. After the court hearings, she didn't stay on to chat with her relatives who came to show their support. She felt she had shamed them and just wanted to go back to the prison. I think the prison also gave her a false sense of security. She would reminisce with me about her time with a group of cellmates who are close to her. She keeps in touch with them mostly over the phone as they are busy with getting their lives back together.

I feel my fellow inmates at Bang Kwang were more honest about their flaws than many supposedly law-abiding citizens I have met on the outside. Everywhere I look now, there are people who try to make money through dishonest means. Changes have to come from the top down. The politicians must stop exploiting the government for personal gain. Then hopefully officers in the civil service and businesspeople will follow.

Although I try not to dwell on the past, I can't help but wonder was Mong the unnamed informant Amnat talked about? Did he supply Amnat with our information? If so, did Amnat use it to plot against us? I'm not sure if answers to these questions would ease our pain. I never entertain myself with thoughts of receiving compensation and neither does Nok.

To my mind, there is no way to put a price on the time lost by two people locked away in their prime. I would rather that apologies were made to those who are suffering. I know what a betrayal it is to be wronged by the officers who have taken an oath to protect and serve you.

Amnat, who framed us, passed away some years ago. The whereabouts of his accomplices are unknown and it isn't my concern. I no longer want revenge but I'll never forgive them. Many things in Thailand have improved much in the past two decades but I'm afraid the same cannot be said for the justice system.

I hope my story will remind everyone that corruption in the police force is a longstanding problem in Thailand as I'm sure it has been elsewhere. I also would like to urge Thai police to recognise what a great responsibility they have and to live up to expectations. I sincerely hope that one day the Thai people can call them *pupitak santirat* (keepers of public peace) with less hesitation.

I believe no judicial system in the world is flawless, whether here or in the west. I'm against the use of the death penalty anywhere in the world for this reason. There is always a chance, no matter how slim it is, of killing an innocent person.

Chapter 8 ❧

LOVE BEHIND BARS

I guess it's true when they say people find love in the strangest places. I would like to introduce you to a Thai woman named Narisa. She is one of the few people to make it their personal mission to help the inmates at Bang Kwang. During my last years there, I saw Thais picketing in front of the prison to protest against the death penalty from time to time but Narisa has done much more. She has been visiting Thai and foreign inmates for many years. She even fell in love with one, a German called Jacomo.

What makes her even more special is the fact that she married him. Somehow they managed to have a wedding behind bars, even though the institution's rules do not recognise romances that bloom there. I sat down with her to talk about her union with Jacomo and what motivates her to help those the general public view as undeserving. This is her story:

❧ ❧ ❧

When I was a child, I used to visit Buddhist temples with my grandmother regularly. While she chatted with her friends or monks, I played with the temple boys. Although running around with them in my long skirt wasn't easy, I had fun. I grew up in a traditional household with three sisters and we were as polite as Thai girls should be, especially in the presence of adults. However, deep down I had a side to me that one might call adventurous. I wanted to know more and to get out of my comfort zone sometimes.

I was a little girl in 1973 when the October bloodbath took place in Bangkok. University students and others demonstrated against the dictatorship near the Democracy Monument. I despised the soldiers who opened fire, killing dozens of protesters. It shocked me to the core and I no longer thought of my country the same way.

I graduated from university in Bangkok with a degree in English and theatre arts. My first job was as a reporter at a Japanese news bureau in the capital covering politics, the army and foreign affairs. That time opened my eyes to aspects of my country that I had been ignorant of. I learnt about self-censorship and what the media can and cannot report on in Thailand. Although press freedom was limited, I felt very alive doing my job. I travelled a lot and to places where I couldn't have gone otherwise.

I visited army camps at the borders. Seeing how hard these soldiers worked changed my attitude towards them. They lived in bad conditions and ran the risk of stepping on landmines. I realised how fortunate I was and felt thankful for these brave soldiers. The villagers who lived near the border literally had to run for their lives dodging bullets when armed conflict took place. My heart ached for these people who had to deal with this every day. Those who had it the worst were the Cambodian and Lao immigrants. Some of them had nothing to sleep on but the bare ground. In the rainy season, they huddled under plastic sheeting that barely kept off the rain or the strong winds.

This humbling experience made me more acutely aware of the ugly truth about some politicians who exploited government projects for monetary gain. I couldn't help but feel disgust when comparing the soldiers and villagers to these corrupt people. They do whatever it takes to get what they want, which is either more money or more power, or both. Their greed seems to know no bounds.

Working as a serious journalist can make you feel frustrated at the illnesses of society. I was made aware of inconvenient truths and it made me determined to change society. There was always one question at the back of my mind: what we are here for—to step over each other for transient wealth and fame? I don't think either wealth or fame can make a person really happy.

For as long as I can remember, I have believed that, besides my parents, there is something else that protects and helps me. I didn't know what it was but I wanted to find out. I refused to think of life as a cycle of birth, study, work, marriage, ageing and death. Life had to be more than that, I thought.

The chance for change came to me when I least expected it. On my way to a piano class, while passing through Siam Square, a little western girl said to me, 'Would you like to give a donation for love?'

It was different from what I was used to hearing from temples where monks promise to improve everything about you in exchange for alms. I gave her a small amount and we began to talk about Jesus. Near the end of our conversation, she said she wanted to make sure that Christ would remain in my heart, so we prayed together. I forgot about the little angel until I received a letter from her. Soon after, I met with her missionary mother, who said to me, 'Are you looking for freedom?'

Her question struck a chord with me and she gave me a Bible. I was familiar with some of biblical verses from reading the works of William Shakespeare but none had left any real impression on me. Then while reading the Bible I found this, 'Where the Spirit of the Lord is, there is liberty.' Continuing slowly and attentively, I rediscovered what I had felt as a child: that something protects me besides my parents. That something is God and this realisation set me free from all my fears now that I knew where I had begun and where I would end. I believe God guides and has predestined my life.

I decided to quit journalism to start a new life that would be spent caring for others. People who knew me were shocked because I was doing well at work but I don't regret my choice at all. I joined a missionary group and it was an experience no amount of money could buy.

As a full-time volunteer, I met troubled people from every walk of life, each with their own set of problem. They all seemed to yearn for the same thing: love from their loved ones or just from another human being.

I realised that if I wished to change society, I had to be that change myself. After all, I have full control only over what I do. I think if I can inspire another person for the better, then it is worth it. You can never know how many lives will be changed by one good example.

I became good friends with Susan 'Dusty' Aldous, an Australian co-worker, and we gave ourselves the nicknames Salt and Pepper. Together we worked with Thai officers from government agencies. We complemented each other really well. She is a westerner who can speak and read Thai and I am a Thai who can speak English. Our presence made people we worked with feel comfortable. We worked with youths at a drug rehabilitation centre in Pattaya, with school students and women who had escaped human trafficking.

Once we were filmed by a television station and after that Kru Noi or Nuannoi Timkul, who works with underprivileged children, asked us to help out at her centre. We collected toys, dried food, rice and snacks for the children and gave centre a spring clean as well. The kids helped to repaint the place with us and we had great fun.

Eventually I visited Bang Kwang with Dusty. She had been asked by a friend to visit an American inmate and I decided to tag along. The very name conjures up fear in people's minds and Bang Kwang prisoners are perceived to be the worst kind of criminals. At first, I didn't know what to talk about to them, for fear of making them feel awkward. However, it didn't take me long to realise that they are human beings too. I don't think we should ostracise them forever because of the mistakes they made.

Papa Joe, an African-American, was the first inmate I befriended. He was later transferred to Klong Prem Prison in Bangkok. I knew some Mexican inmates there and we urged them to take good care of him. He served time there for a while before being sent back to America. He did a few months in a US prison before he was released. I never heard from him again.

Some inmates were abrupt at first but when I saw improvements in them because of my persistence it was worth it.

During our first weeks, the guards neither smiled nor talked to us. I think they acted coldly towards us because they didn't know who we were or about the work we had done before. They probably thought we were spying on them to report their misconduct or something. I guess it was hard for them to understand why we had chosen to help the inmates. We gave the guards due courtesy and followed the rules in the hopes of being on friendly terms with them. Eventually I gave up trying to be nice and that was when an official asked me if I was feeling all right because I was very quiet that day. Then I knew we had won them over but they were too proud to come across as too friendly with outsiders.

Once they had got used to us, we started to help the officers to communicate with the families of foreign inmates who came to visit. Most prison guards cannot speak English and this causes misunderstandings between them and the visiting families. Often they are seen as rude and unhelpful. We became unofficial interpreters at the prison, informing the families about prison regulations and protocols.

While Dusty organised projects, such as giving glasses to elderly inmates and making improvements at the prison hospital with help from the authorities, I focused on visiting prisoners and providing interpretation. I also volunteered to be a co-ordinator between foreign inmates, their families and the embassies. The embassy staff didn't visit prisoners as often as I did so it benefited all sides that I acted as a messenger.

When I started going to the prisons, I was allowed to visit different inmates. In my opinion, the westerners are treated better than the Thais. There are many accounts of guards beating Asians while westerners are unlikely to become their targets because they have embassies to protect them.

I was unfortunate enough to come into conflict with a guard who is known for being mean to the inmates and for not getting on with his younger colleagues. He said I had used a room reserved for embassy staff to visit a Polish man without permission. In fact, I had been asked by a representative of his embassy to talk to him so I had the right to use that room. The guard went on to lie that I had used the room to talk with Jacomo and had me banned me from the prison.

I found out about his accusation when an officer handed me a paper to sign which stated that I had violated prison regulations by using the embassy room. I told him there was no way I would dignify the false accusation with my signature. I said, 'May I ask if any of the officials who put their names to this serious accusation against me had verified it? If it is untrue, these officials will be liable for being false witnesses. Please take it back.'

Jacomo was asked to sign a similar statement but he refused to do so. The officers never mentioned it again.

I never thought Jacomo and I would develop a romantic relationship but if God hadn't wanted us to be together, he wouldn't have allowed us to get married inside the prison. I didn't want to wait until Jacomo was free because that would be too long. More importantly, making our union legal makes it easier for me to represent him. It never crossed my mind that he might be using me. We decided to get married because it is what two people do when they love each other. Even though we haven't known each other long or had physical contact, our feelings are real and mutual.

'Don't marry the person you can live with but marry the person you can't live without' pretty much sums up my feelings about him. Thank God the warden of the prison is open-minded and kind. Not only did he give us permission but he also gave us a blessing. It was the first time in Bang Kwang history's that an inmate on death row had got married inside. I joked that Jacomo was a Dead Man Marrying.

Jacomo is an honest, straightforward person and I think that is what landed him in Bang Kwang. He was living in Chiang Mai, where he ran a brick manufacturing firm, when he was arrested for murder.

A Swiss friend, who was leaving the country, asked Jacomo to let another Swiss man stay with him. Jacomo was reluctant to do so as that man had a record of substance abuse. Eventually he agreed to put him up at his office, which was near his house. He didn't pay much heed to the guest and allowed him to come and go as he pleased.

There had been a fire at the office and it was being repainted. Early one morning, the painter called Jacomo over the fence of his house, saying there was something wrong with his guest. One of Jacomo's feet had got burnt during the fire so he picked up his aluminium cane for support and went to the office. There he found the Swiss man curled up in a ball on the floor. He thought the man was drunk and had passed out so he tried to wake him up to tell him to go to sleep in his bedroom.

It turned out that he was dead. Jacomo called a Thai lawyer friend who suggested he call the police. He asked his friend to do it for him because he could't speak Thai. After the police had investigated the scene, he went to the station to give his report and then went home.

Two days later, he went to the police station to ask what he should do next and about the process of investigation.

The police left him waiting until 10pm and then arrested him for murder.

Of course, he was beaten during the infamous police 'investigation' procedures. There is no need to ask whether they demanded money from him and threatened him with all sorts of violence either. As a Thai, I've heard these stories too many times before. It is impossible that different people could come up with so many similar accounts of police brutality.

At the time Jacomo had a casual girlfriend called Duang, who also worked for him. What he did not know was that she was seeing a policeman at the same time. She had told him the policeman was her brother. At the station, that policemen pointed his pistol at Jacomo's forehead and tried to force him to confess to a crime he hadn't committed. While Jacomo was in police custody the girl stole from his home.

After being beaten up, he was left with a black eye and a broken nose. His Thai lawyer couldn't do much to help him because he was under tremendous pressure from the local police. Jacomo had very few witnesses to testify in his favour. Some witnesses were bought off and turned against him. The few who spoke for him were threatened and one was killed. His embassy wasn't helpful and just kept telling him not to worry.

Chiang Mai court sentenced him to death even though they had no proof to link him to the murder. His conviction was based on circumstantial evidence. The witnesses lied that he had a stainless steel cane, when it was a hollow aluminum cane, implying that he used it to kill the Swiss man. The investigators didn't find any scientific evidence or DNA at the crime scene or on the cane.

I believe Jacomo was given the death penalty just because high-ranking police officers wanted to look tough by prosecuting a westerner. He was sent to Bang Kwang immediately. After two years and eight months the Appeal Court reduced his sentence to 15 years but it upheld the first verdict. The very fact that the Appeal Court commuted the death penalty should say something about how questionable the original verdict was.

Jacomo decided not to fight his case in the Supreme Court because it would take years and he would not be eligible for a transfer back to Germany unless his case was finalised. He hopes that when he gets back to Germany he can find a way to overturn the Thai court verdict.

He had been in Bang Kwang for about two years when we met in November 2005. I believe he didn't kill the Swiss man. If he had, wouldn't it have been wiser for him to just run away? The fact that he showed up at the police station two days in a row after he found the body to ask about the case shows he is innocent.

I don't remember how we started to become more than friends. One day I just knew that we were. We started off with the usual topics of conversation and soon I started to notice how his questions were getting more personal, like when he asked what I think about love. Strangely I replied as if I had prepared, 'Love is giving and believing in the one you love.' He replied, 'To me, trust is important and love isn't complete without it.'

He went on to ask why I was not married. I told him frankly, 'I've seen too many couples fail eventually. Don't you think it is boringly strange to wake up and see the same face of the other person every day?' He didn't say anything to that but had an odd look on his face.

I had told him I used to study German some years ago but never got to use it after graduation so it got rusty. Not many Thais are really fluent in German and I was thinking about brushing it up as it could help my career. Jacomo said I should go to the Goethe Institute in Bangkok and offered to pay. I said if I wanted to study German, I would pay for myself.

I forgot about it after that until he brought it up again. He insisted I ask about the syllabus and report back to him. I then knew he was serious about me studying his language. I applied for an email correspondence course, which required me to go to class once a week.

Jacomo's mother came to visit him so I got to practise my half-baked half-forgotten German with her. We managed to communicate, though, because she can speak some English. She noticed that Jacomo thought of me as more than a friend and even told him that I'm the kind of girl she would like to have as a daughter-in-law.

At the beginning of our relationship, Jacomo and I wrote letters to each other because we had so much to talk about visits were not enough. He wrote in German and I replied in English so we could express ourselves best. We wrote pages and I couldn't help but smile while reading them. We talked about everything including matters regarding his case.

After many letters, one day he said, 'Nina, I'm in love with you.' He said he was relieved to be able to say it, adding that it took guts to confess his feelings. 'What do you think of me?' he continued. 'If you don't feel the same, you can tell me so I won't have to waste my time.'

I felt the same but I wanted to ask myself some serious questions first because I didn't want to let him or myself down later. I replied, 'I'm very happy to hear that but I need some time to think about it. I promise you I'll give the answer the next time we meet.'

I was in love with him too but I knew that if I told him that, it would be the first step in a serious relationship. I needed to ask myself whether I could take him seriously and handle the consequences that would surely follow our love. I needed to ask myself how long I could wait for him and whether I would lose confidence in him in the long run? My answer was that I loved him enough to deal with anything that might come between us. I gave my answer to him as promised and we continued to write letters to each other.

About two months later, he proposed to me in German in a letter. 'Would you like to be my wife, in good times, bad times till death do us part?' This time, with immediate confidence, I replied 'yes' in a letter. Then he proposed to me in person again. That was when we started trying to get married behind bars. He said he wanted to get everything done properly but I was not sure if such an arrangement would be allowed because he was on death row.

His mother contacted the embassy, which immediately sent a letter to the prison asking for permission for a wedding. The warden readily gave us permission. He and I submitted every document requested of us by the embassy in Thailand and agencies in Germany as well. It took about eight weeks for them to verify our papers. In the meantime, I visited his mother in Germany. I received word from the embassy two weeks after I returned to Thailand.

After that, we discussed the date of our wedding. We both preferred Friday evening since that is when the prison is less crowded. Nonthaburi city hall received documents from the embassy but hadn't decided on the date. The city chief told us that we could choose the date and assured us that registering a marriage behind bars was not a problem as it is considered an outside service. We proposed 1pm on Monday, December 8, 2008 for the ceremony and the three agencies—the embassy, the prison and the district—all agreed.

I ran around choosing my dress, his suit and the rings. It was a pity that Jacomo could not participate. His only request was that our rings should be gold. I could put any inscription on them. I chose identical rings with a tiny door on each inscribed with the words BIS ZUM ENDE (to the end). When opened, it would reveal our names: mine on his and vice versa.

Having our union recognised by law makes it easier for me to represent him legally. I was very impressed by how opened-minded the warden was. I was fortunate to meet him. He and several other former wardens of Bang

Kwang hoped that nobody would have to be executed during their tenure. I have great respect for him because he didn't control the inmates with force and appeared to have understanding and sympathy for them. The same cannot be said for some of the people who worked under him, unfortunately.

One week before the wedding, I went to Sukhothai to attend the marriage of a childhood friend and her French groom. I had six days of vacation and joined in a merit-making on her birthday before returning to Bangkok in high spirits. The following day I visited Jacomo and I could tell he was as excited as I was.

On the day, I woke up early and went to Dusty's apartment to prepare. I didn't eat much because I was really giddy. I changed into my beautiful dress and had some pictures taken before setting off. I waited for our friends and the officers to arrive at Bang Kwang's foreign affairs office. Four staff from the German embassy came, including the consul. Two officials came from Nonthaburi city hall.

My flower girls were British prison visitors Katherine and Gale. A friendly Thai guard named Joe welcomed us enthusiastically. He said he was happy that a joyous event would happen inside the usually gloomy Bang Kwang. Katherine and Gale presented me with a card, a cake and a violet-and-white bouquet. The city officials came prepared with two identical marriage licences printed on glossy paper. The embassy staff presented me with another bouquet. With two bouquets in my arms, I walked into the prison, hoping Jacomo and I could meet in person with nothing between us for the first time.

Then I was told that the wedding had to be held in the room reserved for embassy staff. It was not what we had expected. Jacomo and I thought we would be able to stand next to each other without mesh or glass between us. I was upset and it showed but I tried not to let this change ruin my special day.

When I entered the room, Jacomo, his best man and witness were there, waiting for us. He beamed with happiness and this put me at ease. He was also upset, however, that we couldn't get married the way we wanted.

Dear Joe was running around trying to find out why the original plan had been changed. He was out of breath when he showed me an internal paper indicating that the guard who tried to have me banned from the prison before had used his authority to object to us holding our wedding behind the second main gate of the prison, where we could have stood next to each other, holding hands. Apparently this piece of information never showed up at the foreign affairs office before and Joe, who works there, found out it existed only minutes before we did.

Jacomo and I had no choice but to communicate by phone with glass between us. At least we could see each other clearly for the first time, I thought. I kept telling myself not to be upset by this bullying guard. When we signed the marriage licence, the two officials, one on my side and the other on his, had to rush in and out to pass papers between us.

Had we been allowed to get married inside as requested, none of this awkwardness would have happened. Did they think I would try to help him to escape? Fortunately, Dusty, Gale and Katherine entertained the witnesses and guests and took turns to taking photographs. After we had finished the paperwork, the staff from Nonthaburi city hall and the embassy excused themselves.

We hadn't exchanged rings yet, however. I noticed there was a little door in the room that opened onto an alley that went past the visiting area. If I could get in there, there would be just mesh between us.

I begged the guard on duty, 'Could you please open that door? We need to exchange the rings.' He knew me and my three girlfriends well so he agreed, but said, 'Please don't take too long. I don't want to get into trouble.'

My girlfriends and I rushed in and everyone sitting in the visiting area seemed to be fixated by the drama Jacomo and I had created. As in many movies, I would like to believe they silently gave us moral support, anticipating a happy ending for a star-crossed couple. We exchanged rings and kissed each other a couple of times through the mesh. The wire was dirty but that was the least of my concerns at that moment. The same official came and asked us politely to go back to the embassy room before any of his supervisors could catch us.

As we walked back to the room, Jacomo shouted, 'How do you feel being my Mrs?' I said, 'Great!' Jacomo and I continued to talk in the embassy room until visiting hours ran out. He told me I should celebrate with the girls and we told him to do the same with his best man. We gave cakes, snacks and drinks to the officials on duty, courtesy of Jacomo. It felt so surreal when I walked out of the prison, knowing that I had just got married yet my husband was still inside. We four girls continued our celebrations until late in the evening. When I got home, I took out the marriage licence and looked at it with equal amounts of delight and bewilderment. I don't know if he had a good sleep the night of our wedding but I did.

Jacomo was still beaming with happiness the next time we met and he asked me how I had celebrated with the girls. He assured me, as always, that I didn't need to worry about him and I should have fun. He said something really sweet then: I should do whatever I felt like while I could because after his release he would try to compensate for his absence by spending most of his time with me.

He said when he proposed to me he felt like I was already an integral part of his life. He used to think that a marriage licence was just a piece of paper but now he felt it cemented our relationship.

I knew our relationship was firmly established before our wedding. The mesh, glass and distance between us couldn't stop me. We cherished every minute we had during the visits. I went to see him even when it was lashing rain. We didn't waste time feeling bitter that we had to meet in this unpleasant place and under such awful circumstances. I didn't pay heed to the guard who tried to stop us. The guards and inmates know how persistent I am. Once I got stuck in traffic because of heavy rain and a 30-minute taxi ride from my home to the prison turned into one hour and 30 minutes but I was determined to keep my word. He told me later that his friends had kept reassuring him that I would come back and when his name was called they let out big cheers.

I don't think the obstacles that have come between us could have stopped our love from growing. We are physically apart but we are together emotionally. I have never thought about stopping visiting him or giving up at all.

His mother was concerned that time would wear down my patience and love for Jacomo and, given the unusual circumstances, she wasn't sure our relationship would be given a chance to mature. For these reasons, she didn't tell his father, whom she had divorced when Jacomo was young, about our union initially.

I tried to contact his father a few times. I wrote to tell him that Jacomo and I had got married but got no reply for over a month. We thought he might not approve of our union until one day he rang me. He said he wasn't able to contact me because his phone was out of order and he was away on holiday for weeks. He didn't make any comment about our wedding at all. A few months later, he called me again after the story of our wedding was published in Germany. He said they used nice picture of me alongside the interview. I've never met him in person but he is always courteous with me over email and phone, though he is a man of few words. I keep him posted about matters regarding Jacomo and me. I'm glad his parents didn't object to our union.

When I told my mother about Jacomo, she said, 'Is he the one?' She said my father believed that as parents they could only raise their children bodily but could not shape our hearts. She assured me, 'No matter what happens, your father and I will be here for you.' It was the best blessing she could have given me.

Perhaps she knew that the wedding was coming. Jacomo had arranged to send flowers to me and my mother on special occasions. I found out later that he asked Gale to send the flowers on his behalf. In Germany, when a guy sends flowers to his girlfriend, he gives some to her mother as well.

I had expected *Mae* would strongly disapprove of my decision to marry him but she let me decide for myself. My mother didn't raise the obvious concern, that Jacomo is behind bars. I thank God that she didn't object to my decision because her blessing means a lot to me. Perhaps she had a similar experience when one of my sisters married a Japanese man.

None of my siblings objected to the marriage either. My sisters teased me that I must have found the right one because I had vowed before never to get married.

Both of us have come a long way. Jacomo used to be very frustrated by the situation and angry that the Thai authorities had made a scapegoat of him. Now he says he understands why he was sent to Bang Kwang. He said to me: 'I thank God. I thank the death sentence and those who put me in this place because they led me to you… but I also want God to help me get out of here. Being in a German prison is not a problem but without you I don't think I can make it through.'

I will move to Germany to be with him after the transfer. He has many plans to get his life back. I've prepared everything for this transition. I completed the basic certificate of German language, which is one of the requirements when applying for an immigrant visa. I have had all the necessary documents translated. With the help of his mother, I believe I will be able to find a job and a house while he is still in jail.

After 10 years as a full-time volunteer, I work freelance now too. I usually spend my afternoons at a studio doing voiceovers and the evenings on translation jobs. Two days a week, I visit the prison. At the weekend, I relax with friends or spend time with inmates' families who are visiting Thailand.

I don't want to call my volunteer work a job because no one pays me to do it. I do it because I have deep sympathy for the prisoners. My 'wages' are the thanks and the happiness I get from helping out.

When people hear I visit prisoners on death row, they usually look puzzled and ask me why I do it. I explain to them that not all inmates are evil and some have been made scapegoats. They are shackled 24 hours a day unless their sentences are commuted to life in prison or less.

They suffer from bruises caused by friction between the heavy iron and their flesh. Those who are lucky enough to have the shackles removed while they are alive must deal with long-term back pain because of the extra weight they were forced to carry around for years. The less fortunate ones have their shackles removed only after death.

This goes against the United Nations' Standard Minimum Rules for the Treatment of Prisoners, which does not allow the use of restraints as punishment. The prison dismisses this by saying inmates on death row are considered high-risk so, under the Thai Corrections Act, they have to be shackled to prevent them from escaping or harming others. The prison also justifies this practice by pointing out that it does not have enough staff to provide control and security.

To brand the inmates on death row as high-risk is punitive. They aren't allowed contact visits, even though they are the ones who need it the most since their relatives don't know when they will be executed. When they are ill, they are rarely sent outside for treatment, for fear they will try to escape.

A lot could be done to improve the system. The real reform has to begin at every police station where brutality is still the norm. Thailand is a Buddhist country yet it imposes the death penalty. Buddhists know that killing is against the very first precept laid down by Buddha for laymen. Some officers who work in Bang Kwang oppose the death penalty and several past wardens didn't want any executions to take place during their tenure.

I think life imprisonment is scarier than death, especially if you have to be in a Thai prison.

I know there are people who intentionally hurt others and they should be dealt with accordingly. But the authorities should recognise that inmates, even those on death row, are human beings too.

In May 2010, Jacomo was transferred back to Lübeck in Germany and Narisa was preparing to join him.

Chapter 9 ❧

BANG KWANG TEMPLE

It is a Buddhist belief that when you do good to another being, the amount of merit you earn depends on how spiritually pure that being is. In short, you earn more merit helping a monk than a layman.

For Thai Buddhists, there will be many occasions throughout life when they need the services of the monks. Expectant parents or those with newborns consult monks before naming their children so as to give them an auspicious start in life. Sons show gratitude towards their parents by becoming monks for a period and, ideally, before they get married as it makes a man more desirable as a husband. Buddhists also call on monks in their later years and when they feel unlucky.

For a fee, they can go to temples that offer a symbolic death and rebirth. By getting into and out of a coffin, while monks chant to safeguard the transition, they can be absolved of bad karma incurred through wrongdoing.

It stays with the former selves they left in the coffins. How convenient.

After death, monks chant while mourners come to pay their respects at funerals, which can take up to five days. Some unorthodox monks have held mass ordinations of former drug addicts to help them to rehabilitate themselves and prepare to return to society. To say that monks are integral and influential members of Thai society is no overstatement.

Temple affairs are a lifelong interest of mine. I have contributed articles about notorious crimes in recent Thai history to Buddhist magazines, where they have run alongside advertisements for amulets, invitations to the consecration of new *stupas*, profiles of monks and stories of personal miracles. I am fortunate to have met several renowned monks who were eager to give me their take on how I became an executioner in my current life. They also impressed me with how they can fill their abodes with earthly possessions and expensive electronics their followers have bestowed upon them.

Some years ago, when a once highly revered monk was sentenced to 160 years in Bang Kwang for sexual offences against nine underage girls, I got the chance to observe an interesting phenomenon I would like to call Bang Kwang Temple. The former abbot maintained his following, despite his conviction, and turned the prison into a temple of sorts. Better known among Thais by his monastic name, Bhavana Buddho, he is called Chamlong Khonsue in prison, though his followers still address him as their 'venerable'. He is unique and is the most influential inmate in the Bangkok Hilton at present.

At the pinnacle of his popularity, Bhavana Buddho was the abbot of a temple called Sam Phran in Nakhon Pathom province. He was renowned for making pilgrimages into the wilder parts of the country, teaching meditation and doing charity work. This attracted streams of Buddhists from across the nation to his temple to make merit, practise meditation and pay him their respects. Like any other famous temple, his offered auspicious items for sale. One in particular was a sticker with a picture of Bhavana Buddho assuming a seated cross-legged meditation posture called lotus under a sunshade. The stickers were very popular among truck- and taxi-drivers, who placed them on their vehicles to ward off road accidents.

Bhavana Buddho was also honorary chairman of a foundation set up in his honour that took care of hill tribe children from remote areas. It was said that during a pilgrimage into the north of Thailand, he met with hill tribe children from Chiang Mai and Mae Hong Son provinces, which border Myanmar. The children were uneducated and at high risk of entering prostitution and the drug trade later as teenagers. This inspired him to establish a foundation to help them.

His adopted *dek chao khao* (hill tribe children) lived beside his temple and they were educated in a bid to prevent them, especially the girls, from being sold into prostitution by their parents. This practice is called *dtok kieow*, which when literally translated means a transaction between a moneylender and a farmer in which the farmer who has unripe rice paddies is given a loan on condition that he repay the moneylender with the produce.

The term is also used to describe a different kind of business deal whereby the parents borrow from a moneylender when their daughter is very young (as green as young rice) on condition that, when she becomes a teenager (ripe), she will leave school prematurely and work as a prostitute to repay the moneylender.

The unexpected fall from grace of Bhavana Buddho began in August 1995 when Kriengsak Bhumirungroj, a male nurse and former follower of the abbot, and Surat, a monk from another temple, brought letters by six hill tribe girls claiming they had been raped by the abbot to the attention of the Religious Affairs Department, the Crime Suppression Division and a child welfare protection unit under the Public Welfare Department. Surat was a relative of one of the victims and he had asked her to write down what had happened.

The accusations were considered outrageous because the abbot presented himself as a protector of children. The news spread rapidly and the media covered the case extensively. The story shook the Buddhist nation to its core. His followers were steadfast and expressed their disapproval of the negative news coverage and sensational headlines. They believed it was a plot to discredit Bhavana Buddho.

Before these allegations came to light, the nation's faith in Buddhism had already been put to the test by a scandal involving a popular monk called Yantra, who was praised widely for his goodness and noble conduct. He was accused of having sexual intercourse with his Thai and foreign female followers while he was a monk in 1994. He was also accused of fathering a daughter and the mother of this child challenged him to a paternity test. At first, Yantra was defended by a prominent religious agency, which believed that a group of American and Thai people was out to destroy Thai Buddhism and had chosen Yantra, then the religion's golden boy, as their prime target.

Eventually, however, Yantra was expelled on the orders of the Sangha Supreme Council. Unwilling to give up completely, he started to wear a dark green robe instead of saffron. When a lawsuit was instigated against him on charges of impersonating a monk, he fled to America. Reportedly he has lived there since and he retains a following.

At the peak of Yantra's popularity, his followers took lotuses to him to bless. They then boiled the flowers in water and drank it to cure illnesses. Some asked him to step on white cloth and then took the dust from his feet home to worship. The Ministry of Education said later that one of his followers was so traumatised by the accusations against Yantra, he had to be hospitalised.

That scandal dealt quite a blow to Thai Buddhism, so it is understandable that the authorities seemed to be slow to instigate a case against Bhavana Buddho. The abbot was a highly respected figure and the police would lose face if they didn't have enough evidence to make charges stick in the court of justice and court of public opinion. Police Major General Kamnueng Thamkasem, then commandant of the Crime Suppression Division, entrusted Police Colonel Nukul Sompat, his deputy, to lead an investigation into the allegations. The reputation of the national religion was at stake.

In the meantime, a report surfaced about a high-ranking state officer's attempt to pull strings with the police to get the abbot out of this difficulty. The abbot disappeared from the public eye and was rumoured to have fled the country.

Police Colonel Nukul said his investigation team contacted the Department of Religion for information about the rape claims before a team was dispatched to Chiang Mai province and Mae Song Son province to gather more details. There they met six girls who said they had been raped by the abbot in his quarters. They were all under 15.

In an interview, Nukul said it took time to persuade the girls' parents to allow their children to give statements. This is what the police were told eventually, he said: 'Under pretence of a request to clean the room, the girls were lured in. Then Bhavana Buddho would ask the girls to give him a massage. He told them that touching him wouldn't bring bad karma onto them (because Buddhism forbids physical contact between monks and females). In the middle of the massage, he forced himself on them. Should a girl resist, he would remind her of the favours he had done for her.'

To avoid being seen entering his room, the girls were instructed to go through a secret door, which could be accessed by ladder only.

Eventually a joint force of 60 from the Crime Suppression Division and the provincial police of Nakhon Pathom went to Sam Phran Temple to conduct an investigation. They discovered girls' hair in the air-conditioner. They didn't find the secret door but found traces of a ladder, which led them to conclude that the place had been changed before their arrival to rid it of evidence that might incriminate the abbot. Medical examinations confirmed that the girls had been sexually violated. A warrant for the abbot was issued.

As if that were not shocking enough, seven Buddhist nuns living at his temple were accused of procuring young girls for him. The idea that these nuns, who were aged between 18 and 27, were acting as *mamasans* sent another shock wave across the nation.

A second, more sordid version of the story was used in subsequent court hearings. The nuns were said to lead the girls one by one to the abbot's residence through an adjoining toilet to clean the room. Once inside, the girls said they were told by the nuns to pay their respects to a Buddha figure as the abbot walked down from upstairs. The abbot then told the girls to bow at his lap as he stroked their hair. He then asked them to either make his bed or give him a massage; again in the court hearings they said he assured them they would not bring bad karma on themselves by touching him. Then he forced himself on the girls.

First, he embraced them from behind as the nuns took hold of their arms and legs before he caressed their breasts and penetrated them. After he finished, the girls were told to take contraceptive pills and wash their private parts thoroughly before the nuns led them away. If a girl refused to have sexual intercourse with the abbot, she would be punished by being forced to walk slowly on a path covered with sharp pebbles under the glaring sun.

Bhavana Buddho eventually turned himself in to the Crime Suppression Division accompanied by a few followers. The seven nuns were accused of procuring nine girls for the abbot. The nuns became defendants number two to eight while Bhavana Buddho was defendant number one.

During the long-running legal case, Bhavana Buddho and the nuns were granted bail and continued to live at Sam Phran Temple. The trial took an unusually long time because of the many people concerned with the case and the numerous requests for deferment from both the defence and the prosecution. There were also several witnesses who lived in the north of Thailand and it was difficult for them to come to the police to give their statements. After the police found out that the witnesses who testified for the victims had been threatened, Bhavana Buddho was forced to give up his position as a monk and fight the case as a layman under his own name, Chamlong Khonsue.

On June 21, 2004, nine years after the allegations hit the headlines, the Criminal Court found the former abbot guilty and sentenced him to 160 years in jail for raping nine underage girls while he was a monk. The attacks were believed to have taken place between August 1988 and January 1995, though there were no exact dates. His sentence was commuted to 50 years. As he was 55 years old at the time, only if he is gifted with great longevity will he serve the full term. He appeared throughout the trial in a brown robe instead of the saffron worn by monks.

Six of the seven former nuns were found guilty and sentenced to jail terms ranging from three to 31 years. Charges against the last defendant were dropped. Defendant number five, who was given three years, didn't seek leave to appeal.

After the trial, Chamlong and five of the female convicts said they planned to appeal and requested bail with 22 million baht worth of land deeds for property in Nakhon Pathom province. He was later sent to Bang Kwang.

That is when Bang Kwang first played host to groups of monks, nuns and lay people dressed in white coming to visit the former abbot. It is a strange sight for a place like this. They address Chamlong with reverence, pay their respects and generously donate money into his prisoner account. Their presence serves as a silent protest against the court's verdict.

Some say these devotees are blinded by their faith and that it is a cult of personality. The followers certainly regard Chamlong as their abbot. They sit on the bare concrete floor before him because, even dressed in his brown prison uniform, they believe he is holier than they are. Chamlong keeps his monastic appearance as much as he can by shaving his head and eyebrows and always greeting his visitors with a smile.

On one occasion, I heard him instructing his followers to comply with the prison rules and not to argue with the guards after he had learned that there had been heated disagreements between them. He told them, 'Living here makes me realise there are many inmates who suffer much more than I do. If you, my advocates, are interested in giving them some relief please donate 108 baht and I will see to it personally that they receive your kindness.' In his 'sermons', Chamlong told his visitors to pray, abide by Buddha's precepts and frequent temples. The sermons were followed by inquiries from the visitors about his wellbeing, to which he always replied, '*Sabaidee*. Don't worry about me.'

Each time, before the session ended, he blessed them as if he were still wearing the sacred saffron robe, while they bowed their heads to him with their hands joined in prayer. To ask for a blessing from a convict is incomprehensible to most Thais, but not these followers. Elated by the meeting, each of them seemed to glow with an internal light or to have tears in their eyes.

Not everybody saw goodness, however, and a nasty rumour circulated in prison that Chamlong had deflowered the hill tribe girls in his efforts to attain the highest level in his pursuit of supernatural power.

One anonymous male follower said in an interview, 'I'm saddened that he has to go through this ordeal even though he has done nothing wrong. He told us he doesn't want to protest his innocence, saying he cannot achieve *baramee* (virtue prestige) without the challenge of evil. I believe this ordeal serves as a test for him to gain enlightenment (which could lead one to being free from the cycle of rebirth—the highest goal in Buddhism). It's like he is now in jail to preach to hellish creatures.'

His analogy is derived from a Buddhist tale, created around 357 by a Singhalese monk, about another monk named Phra Malai who frequented hell so that he could give the tormented souls a temporary reprieve and to preach to them. Clearly Chamlong's follower was comparing Bang Kwang to hell on earth and prisoners as creatures from hell who are suffering as result of their own karma.

He continued: 'Prior to the verdict, I had been praying for him and extending my well wishes towards him in the hopes that he would be cleared of the charges. I was distraught to learn that it turned out to be the exact opposite of what I hoped. My daughter doesn't understand why our abbot is in jail. I don't believe he has committed the crimes for which he is being punished. He is a victim of a conspiracy. I will continue to abide by his teachings and apply them to my daily life.'

The prison superintendent gives Chamlong's followers permission to visit him to avoid a conflict, although the fact that they visit him in a big group does not comply with the usual prison rules.

On November 16, 2005, Chamlong was transferred from Bang Kwang to the Criminal Court on

Ratchadapisek Road in Bangkok for a reading of the Appeal Court's verdict. About 300 followers, 15 monks and a few nuns showed up to give him moral support. The court ruled against him, saying the evidence was indisputable. Chamlong purported to be a noble monk while he overindulged in sexual pleasure and exploited his followers, it said.

Chamlong argued that people who opposed him, who he believed to be Christians and animists, had framed him out of jealousy of his popularity. He also said the girls had not fully reached puberty and, therefore, their vaginas were too small for him to possibly penetrate with his uncircumcised penis. The court dismissed his arguments.

The most shocking admission of all came from defendant number two, who was given 31 years in jail. She admitted having sexual intercourse with Chamlong while he was a monk and afterwards procuring young girls for him. She had chosen to remain silent about his transgression for almost a decade for fear of retaliation and out of gratitude since he was paying for her education until she finished a degree. No doubt this admission sealed their fates.

The Appeal Court upheld the jail terms levied on the former abbot and five former nuns. The court ruled the girls had been violated many times and they had no motive to falsely accuse Chamlong, because they were in his care. The girls also were able to give descriptions of his residence, although it was supposed to be private. As for defendants number two to seven, the court ruled that they became his accomplices to protect their own interests and to maintain their status.

During the two-hour reading of the verdict, his followers meditated, prayed and some covered their ears. Upon hearing the final verdict, some broke into tears. Afterwards, the monks and nuns performed a merit-making ritual for Chamlong in front of the Criminal Court. He blessed his followers, asked them not to worry about him and promised to be their spiritual guide regardless of the court's decision. Chamlong and another former nun, defendant number three who was given 28 years, decided to continue to fight their case in the Supreme Court. His followers' faith in him remained intact and they continued to visit him at the prison.

A Spanish woman named Aina not only believes that Chamlong is innocent but also that he was framed for raping the girls in a conspiracy against him that continues. She claimed that a group of people, who were exploiting his incarceration for personal gain, tried to prevent her from helping him. I didn't become interested in her story until she had a disagreement with a guard in charge of visitors. This introduced another layer of complexity surrounding the former abbot.

This is what Aina told me: 'A nun confided in me that, upon the abbot's request, she went to Mae Hong Son to meet the girls who said they had been raped. She went door to door to confront these girls and one of them retorted, "How much money is the monk willing to give me? If he gives me more than I was paid to write the letter (of accusation), then I might consider it." The nun begged the girls to come clean but to no avail. When I asked why she hadn't taken this information to the lawyer or someone who could help the abbot, the nun said, "It's his karma and we cannot do anything to help him."'

Aina believed one of the abbot's followers had framed him so as to gain full control of the donations coming into the temple. Aina said that whenever another follower tried to recommend a lawyer to the abbot, that woman would put forward her choice and this resulted in many changes of lawyer, reducing the abbot's chances of winning the case. Aina said, 'I believe that the Supreme Court will uphold the verdict of the lower courts and his last hope is a sentence reduction by royal pardon.'

Aina was born into a Christian household to a faith-healer father and a secular mother. Her parents' different outlook on life drove them apart. Her mother didn't want to make their house a hospital and her father travelled extensively to heal people. They separated when Aina was seven. However, her father's success in healing people contributed to her decision to become a psychologist and embark on a lifelong quest to be master of her own mind.

She married and had a daughter but divorced her husband after she found out that he had cheated on her. While she was practising as a clinical psychologist and pursuing a master's degree in family psychology, a friend introduced raja yoga to her. She decided to embark on a spiritual journey in India with her daughter so she could learn from the real masters. Her pilgrimage was inspired by the trip to India her favourite thinker Carl Jung had taken.

While in India, she went to mosques, ashrams and temples to learn from the masters of all faiths. In Madras, she met Santi, a Thai monk and disciple of Bhavana Buddho, who was there studying a master's degree in philosophy. Santi asked for permission from his master to resign from the monkhood so he could become Aina's husband. They went back to Spain before travelling to Thailand in early 2004 to meet Bhavana Buddho. She stayed at Sam Phran Temple where she taught the girls about Buddhism in English while Santi helped out at the temple. She has two sons with him.

After Bhavana Buddho was jailed, Santi and Aina came to Bang Kwang to visit him along with the other followers. That was fine—until she started to visit other foreign inmates she met inside. She used to bring her two young sons to prison with her while visiting inmates as well. Before she was banned from the prison, according to the visitors' records, she had seen a Thai, a Singaporean, an Indian and intended to visit a Pakistani.

One could argue that she was just being charitable extending her help to them but, given the fact that they were drug offenders, the officials grew concerned. Two of them were serving life sentences and were considered high-risk inmates. Plus, she was not related to any of them, nor was she a member of a lawfully recognised religious organisation, nor was she a representative of an embassy. To make matters worse, Aina declared her love for an Asian named Chen whom she met when he was inside and claimed that they were spiritually married. Chen was a drug offender and sentenced to life in prison. Previously, he had been held in another Thai jail for a different crime.

Chen's father met Aina while he was registering to visit his son for the first time at Bang Kwang. Aina helped him with the protocol of registration. Afterwards he asked her to visit Chen on his behalf as it cost him a lot to travel to Thailand to visit his son. The family also sent a letter to their embassy in Bangkok to declare Aina as their representative and state that they recognised her as Chen's future wife.

Recalling the day that she was banned from the prison, Aina said, 'The officer who is in charge of visiting rudely said to me, "You no wife. Your country's... very dangerous. Drugs. You no come!" Although my country is known for its cocaine trade, he has no grounds to assume that I'm involved in the drug trade.'

The officials always look at the visitors' log for signs of suspicious activity. They want to reduce the chances of illegal dealings being conducted through the bars. Aina's habits came into question when she visited drug offenders whom she had no business with in the first place. She lodged complaints against the official who banned her with various government agencies, saying she was a target of prejudice. Around the same time, however, a Thai woman who represented the group of Chamlong's followers sent a letter to the authorities saying they disowned Aina because of her suspicious visits with these inmates. Aina had to move out of Sam Phran Temple into an apartment near Bang Kwang paid for by Santi, who now works in a Buddhist temple in America. She presented the authorities with a divorce paper which declared her union with Santi was no more and she asked for permission to marry Chen inside the prison—but to no avail. She even drew up a marriage licence herself between her and Chen. Once she sat in my office after she was denied a visit with Chen. It was raining and, without a hint of irony, she said, 'The sky is crying with me.'

Aina wasn't winning over Thai officials and represented a threat to some of them, though I considered her harmless. Her circumstances were more complicated than others and we had grounds to be concerned. How could we ban her for violating the regulations regarding inmate visits, however, when there were plenty of others who did not conform, such as Chamlong's big groups of followers or the backpackers who stopped by for thrills?

Eventually a compromise was reached and Aina was allowed to visit Chen on condition that she follow the prison rules and not take along her two young sons. She said she was very grateful for the permission.

Although Chamlong's followers did not want to be associated with her, some of them shared her view that he was the victim of an ongoing conspiracy by an insider.

One of Chamlong's Thai female devotees, who preferred to be anonymous, said: 'It's feasible that someone framed him for their own benefit. Millions of baht were donated to him by us visitors. I wonder who is taking care of it now… I've been visiting him at the prison for a long time and what I've seen is too many changes of lawyers working on his case. The lawyers seemed to vie to represent him as there are hefty fees involved but it turns out their only real interest is in getting paid without putting in real work in defending Chamlong. To me, the lawyers are like vultures picking on a dying animal for the best pieces of meat. The followers who try to help him come into conflict with each other as they want the abbot to use their nominated lawyer.'

That follower has a theory as to who wanted to harm the abbot, but no proof, she says. 'I have an insider in mind… All I can speculate is that this person wants total control over the donation money.

'Mind you, the abbot has never been one who uses money for himself. He buys instant noodles and gives them away to his cellmates. He reminds us to count our blessings. Small things we usually take for granted, like noodle sprinkled with chilli, are delicacies to the inmates. Fed up with infighting between us, the abbot told us to let him be. This was bad news for those who wanted to make money from his ordeal. During most of our visits, instead of being bitter about his fate, the abbot told us how he has persuaded inmates to follow the rightful path of Buddhism by ordaining them. Wherever he is, he can make it holy. The fact that he has taken it upon himself to clean the prison reinforces my faith in him all the more. We followers believe he is innocent and perhaps his ordeal has been brought on him by transgressions he committed in his previous life.'

While the rest of Thailand sees Chamlong as a sexual predator, his followers describe him as an innocent victim who accepts his ordeal as a test he has to pass in order to advance up a spiritual ladder. The stark contrast between the two sides of the same story is fascinating to me.

Almost 14 years after the rape allegation came to light, the judge read the verdict of the Supreme Court at Ratchada Criminal Court on May 7, 2009. In court, Chamlong pointed out he was renowned for meditation as a monk. His foundation was recruiting the hill tribe girls for Buddhism from Christianity or animism, however, and this had upset other faith-based organisations, which plotted to destroy him. Another argument the former abbot made was that his penis was abnormal, so he could not perform sexually. The court found his claims inadequate and upheld the 50-year sentence. Chamlong looked solemn while being escorted back to Bang Kwang as his followers knelt down and put their hands together in prayer.

At the time of writing, dozens of white-clad followers still visit him to listen to his teaching for about an hour every Tuesday and Thursday, as if the Bangkok Hilton were a temple. Before they go into the prison to meet him, they usually line up to donate money into his prison account. Each gives either 108 baht or 227 baht as the two numbers are auspicious in Buddhism: 108 refers to 108 omens and 227 refers to the number of precepts laid down by Buddha for the monks to follow. Ironically, Chamlong was found guilty of breaking the very first precept.

One news report ran a rough calculation of Chamlong's wealth. Provided that no fewer than 60 visitors meet him at a time on average, the total amount of money that is put into his account per visit easily comes to 7,000 baht. The report claims he has accumulated 14 million baht in his account, making him the richest prisoner in Bang Kwang.

I don't have a problem with people coming to the prison to listen to teachings but what concerns me is that allowing Chamlong to receive lots of visitors and to be charitable towards his fellow inmates has already made him very influential. The guards have enough influential inmates to deal with already.

In life, there are questions that forever remain unanswered and, to some, the question of Chamlong's innocence is one of them. What is definite is that, over the 30 years of working in Bang Kwang, I have never met an inmate who came to his power the way he did. I'm also amazed by how Chamlong manages to maintain his followers without a temple and, if karma does exist, the good deeds he must have done that warrant him better living conditions in Bang Kwang. Perhaps, the best way to be constructive is to blind oneself, as do his followers, to the crimes the former abbot was found guilty of and choose to listen only to the good teaching he delivers.

Monks indeed are beacons of light for Thai people. With their status, the public gives them respect and trust. When they betray that trust, they must be dealt with accordingly. After all, a saffron robe doesn't make one holy. It is one's conduct that does. As clichéd as it sounds, there are good and bad people in every path of life—even one that is supposed to lead to holiness.

EPILOGUE

I was diagnosed with colonic cancer halfway through the course of preparing this book. I underwent two operations to remove the parts of my intestine that were affected and a subsequent course of chemotherapy.

This makes me think about death but not in the way you might expect. I can honestly say that I prepared for it mentally a long time ago, given what I saw during my years as executioner. I am also financially prepared so I will depart knowing everyone in my family knows that I am ready.

This sets me thinking of the 55 deaths for which I was responsible, however. I meant them no harm but that sounds absurd because I was sanctioned to kill them. I trained my mind to focus on the task in front of me and, although that may sound like I treated them as numbers, I didn't. It was a job no one wanted to do but someone had to and it happened to be me.

I guess what I'm trying to say is that I can only imagine what kind of trauma they went through. They didn't have a chance to say goodbye to their loved ones in person and they didn't know beforehand when they would be executed. I've been given notice that I may 'go' some time soon. I am surrounded by good people who care about me. The more I compare my fate to theirs, the more I want to ask them for forgiveness. I dedicate any goodness that may be borne out of this book entirely to them.

I read the other day that one of the two drug convicts who were executed by lethal injection in recent years grabbed onto the saffron robe of the monk who was performing a last ceremony for them. The monk said the other man was crying. Their bodies were carried out of the prison to the adjoining temple the following day through a small door called the ghost door. A teacher brought 80 students to watch as their bodies were being carried out to teach them about karma. I hope that it will be the last thing about execution on the news for many years to come.

I find being a guitar-playing grandpa a joy. I know my body is deteriorating but that's okay. All the pain and discomfort I feel is taken away as I see my niece growing up or smiling. My wife Tew minds what I eat all the time now. She is my lifelong companion and I am grateful to have her in my life. I don't worry about my three children any more as they are all grown up and are capable of taking care of themselves.

Things change as time goes. People come and go. I don't know what I will be in the next life. But I can honestly say that I am ready.